G000140032

Easy Web Pubиsnıng with HTML 3.2

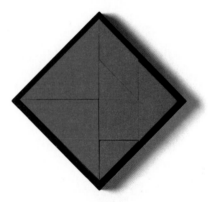

Jonah Neugass

Easy Web Publishing with HTML 3.2

Copyright © 1997 Que® Corporation

All rights reserved. No part of this book shall be reproduced, stored in a retrieval system, or transmitted by any means, electronic, mechanical, photocopying, recording, or otherwise, without written permission from the publisher. No patent liability is assumed with respect to the use of the information contained herein. While every precaution has been taken in the preparation of this book, the publisher and author assume no responsibility for errors or omissions. Neither is any liability assumed for damages resulting from the use of the information contained herein. For information, address Que Corporation, 201 West 103rd Street, Indianapolis, IN 46290. You can reach Que's direct sales line by calling 1-800-428-5331.

Library of Congress Catalog Card Number: 97-65025

International Standard Book Number: 0-29236-1143-5

00   99   98   97   8   7   6   5   4   3   2   1

Interpretation of the printing code: the rightmost double-digit number is the year of the book's first printing; the rightmost single-digit number is the number of the book's printing. For example, a printing code of 97-1 shows that this copy of the book was printed during the first printing of the book in 1997.

Screen reproductions in this book were created by means of the program Collage Complete from Inner Media, Inc, Hollis, NH.

Printed in the United States of America

Dedication

This book is dedicated to my beautiful, sweet, and wonderful wife Amy. Thanks for putting up with me for so long.

Credits

Publisher
Roland Elgey

Publishing Manager
Stacy Hiquet

Editorial Services Director
Elizabeth Keaffaber

Managing Editor
Sandy Doell

Director of Marketing
Lynn E. Zingraf

Acquisitions Editor
Philip Wescott

Technical Specialist
Nadeem Muhammed

Product Development Specialist
Stephen L. Miller

Technical Editor
Bill Bruns
Stephen Gershik

Production Editor
Tonya Maddox

Book Designers
Barbara Kordesh
Ruth Harvey

Cover Designers
Dan Armstrong
Kim Scott

Production Team
Jason Carr, Trey Frank, Amy Gornik,
Christy Hendershot, Bob LaRoche,
Tony McDonald, Kaylene Riemen,
Julie Searls

Indexer
Nick Schroeder

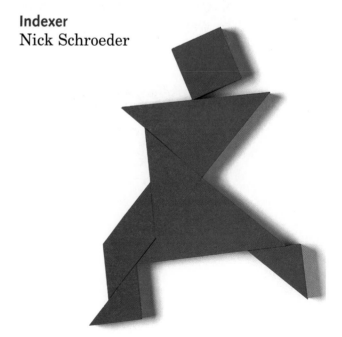

Composed in *Syntax* and *New Century Schoolbook* by Que Corporation

About the Author

Jonah Neugass is currently studying computer science and engineering at Northern Arizona University in Flagstaff, Arizona. He hopes to graduate before the year 2000 and will probably go to work for Jet Propulsion Laboratory, where he spends his summers. Jonah's hobbies include fencing, rollerblading, computers (obviously), and playing lots of games. His wife, Amy, currently resides in Tucson, Arizona, where she is studying to be a radiological technician. Jonah can be reached at **jgn@pine. cse. nau.edu**, and if you wish to check out his home page (which he really needs to work on), it can be found at **na.uc http://dac.nau.edu**.

Acknowledgments

I would like to thank the following people for helping me with this book. First, thanks to Philip Wescott for offering me my first book deal and taking a chance on an unknown college student. Also, thanks to Stephen Miller for keeping me straight on what I needed to do and answering all my questions. Thanks to Tonya Maddox for fixing all my silly mistakes and offering many good suggestions. Finally, I would like to offer thanks to Warren Ernst, for without Warren's help, I would still be buying books from Que instead of writing them.

Trademarks

All terms mentioned in this book that are known to be trademarks or service marks have been appropriately capitalized. Que Corporation cannot attest to the accuracy of this information. Use of a term in this book should not be regarded as affecting the validity of any trademark or service mark.

Contents

Contents

Part IX: Adding Scrolling Messages and Animated GIFs 130

Part X: WebSite Creation Tools and Cool Web Sites 152

Introduction

What You Can Do with HTML

HTML is the language that the World Wide Web is based on today. Many people shy away from HTML because they think of it as programming, but the truth of the matter is that it is actually a set of tags that tell Web browsers, such as Netscape, how to format the text and graphics located in an HTML file. There are thousands of new Web pages each day. Hopefully, yours will be the next.

Here are some specific tasks you will learn how to accomplish with HTML:

- *Create your first Web page.* Your first Web page will show you how to add the following to your page: text, different sized headings, paragraph separators, and horizontal lines. All of these items are covered in Part I, "Basic Web Page Creation."

- *The missing links.* You have your basic page, but now what? You can add "links" to your home page which, when clicked, connect browsers of your page to other pages (including your own). You can learn how to add links in Part II, "Links and Navigation."

- *Fun with graphics.* The Web would not be very interesting if all pages consisted of text only. That is why most Web browsers support several different types of graphics formats. Part III, "Adding Graphics to Your Pages," will show you how to spice up your page with pictures.

- *Make a List.* Lists are one of the ways HTML lets you organize information on your Web pages. You can see how to add several types of lists to your page in Part IV, "Organizing Pages with Lists."

- *Your regular table?* The second major way of organizing data with HTML is with tables. Tables are covered in Part V, "Organizing Pages with Tables."

- *Framing your page.* One of the newest additions to HTML is frames. Frames let you divide the screen into several different parts, each with its own page, letting you create interesting layouts. Part VI, "Cool Page Layout with Frames," covers frames.

- *Setting up links in an Imagemap.* Making one graphic contain several different links is an easy way to show the reader where he or she goes when clicking that part of the graphic. If you show a graphic of the United States, for example, each state could be its own link. Part VII, "Creating an Imagemap," shows you how to create an imagemap for your Web page.

- *Who's visiting my page?* Once you have created your Web page, you need to know how to upload it so people can access it. Uploading your page is explained in this section. Once your page is available, the ability to track how many people have visited your site and who the visitors are is interesting to track. Part VIII, "Uploading Your Web Page to Add Hit Counters and Guestbooks," covers how to get your page uploaded and how to track who is accessing it.

- *Animations and Scrolling Test.* Adding an animated GIF or scrolling text to your Web page really makes your page get noticed. Part IX, "Adding Scrolling Messages and Animated GIFs," shows you how easy it is to add these eye catching features to your Web page.

- *The right tools for the job.* There are some really great tools available as shareware or for free that can help you with the different tasks you need to perform to create a Web page. This part shows you what some of the best ones are and where to get them. The end of this part lists some of the best designed Web pages on the Web. Seeing some of the best pages will give you some ideas of your own to create a great Web page of your own. Part X, "Web Creation Tools and Cool Web Sites," shows you some of the best Web programming tools and sites available today.

Right now you may find it hard to believe that you will be able to perform all this HTML wizardry, but don't worry, with a little time, you will be creating dazzling Web pages on your own!

PART I

Basic Web Page Creation

1 Starting WordPad

2 Learning *<html>*, *<head>*, *<title>*, and *<body>* Tags

3 The Header Tags

4 The *<p>* and *
* Tags

5 Learning Text Alignment

6 Changing the Background Color

7 Changing the Text Color

8 Separating Text with the *<hr>* Tag

9 Emphasizing Text with *<b>* and *<i>* Tags

PART I OF THIS BOOK INTRODUCES you to HyperText Markup Language (HTML, for short). This part shows you the basic steps needed to get your first home page on the World Wide Web.

HTML is what makes up most of the World Wide Web's content. Rather than a real programming language, HTML is a set of *tags* that tells a Web browser how to display an item. For example, the following would make the word "Cool" appear centered in the middle of the page:

```
<b> Cool </b>
```

The first tag, `<b>`, tells the browser that all text that follows will be made bold. The browser knows when to stop "bolding" words when it comes across the `</b>` tag. The `< >` and `</ >` format works like an off and on switch. The first tag tells the browser to turn on a format, the second tells it to stop. There are some tags that do not need a *closing* tag, but adding one just in case won't hurt.

Here are the tags covered in Part I:

`<html>`	The first tag on the page. It tells the browser that the document it is reading is an HTML document. Terminated with `</html>` (the last tag on the page).
`<head>`	Does not have a visible effect on the Web page, but is used to contain important information about the page (such as the title). The `<head>` tag might also contain tags that may help search engines locate your Web site. Terminated with `</head>`.
`<title>`	Used to insert a title that will usually appear at the top of the browser in the title bar. Terminated with `</title>`.
`<body>`	Usually contains all of the text and images that make up a Web page. Terminated with `</body>`.

`<h1>` through `<h5>`	Used for headings. The largest of these heading tags is `<h1>`. They decrease in size all the way to the smallest, `<h5>`. `<h1>` is terminated with `</h1>` (the same follows for the rest of the heading tags).
`<p>` and ` `	Used to help format a body of text. The `<p>` tag specifies that a new paragraph is to be started. The ` ` tag tells the browser to start a new line at a given point. Neither tag needs to be terminated.
`<hr>`	Used to insert a horizontal line onto your Web page. Does not need termination.
`<b>` and `<i>`	Used to make text bold or italic. Terminated with `</b>` and `</i>`.

You are just about ready to create your first Web page, but first you need the following items:

- A computer with Windows 3.1 with 8M of RAM and 5M of hard drive space, or Windows 95 with 8M of RAM and about 10M of hard drive space (or a PowerMac with the same amount of RAM and available HD space, running System 7.5)

- A working modem and an Internet account

- A text editor such as NotePad or WordPad

- A Web Browser (I would suggest Netscape Navigator 3.0 or Microsoft's Internet Explorer)

Once you have your software and Internet connection set up, you are ready to start your first Web page!

`<center> - - -          <center>`

→ `<p align = center>` Another way to center text `</p>`   (using /p tag)
align

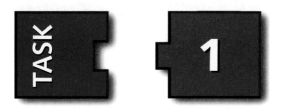

TASK **1**

Starting WordPad

"Why would I do this?"

To start your page, you first open your text editor. This is the program that you use to create all of your HTML files.

Throughout this book you use WordPad to create your HTML files. If you are using another text editor, don't worry! Almost all the steps should be the same (with the possible exception of saving files and copying and pasting text). If you are using Windows 3.1, use NotePad (in the Accessories menu) instead; also, for all you Macintosh users out there, the editor SimpleText will work to create your Web pages.

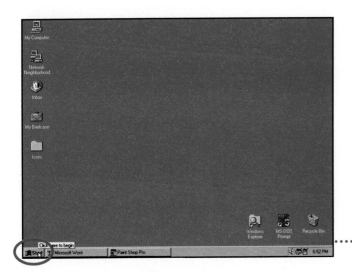

1 To open WordPad, open the **Start** menu.

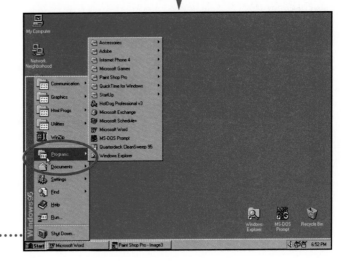

2 Next, move up the Start menu until your cursor highlights the **Programs** folder.

3 Move the cursor up and to the right until the Accessories folder is highlighted.

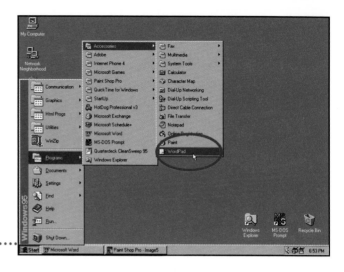

4 Finally, choose **WordPad**, which is down and to the right.

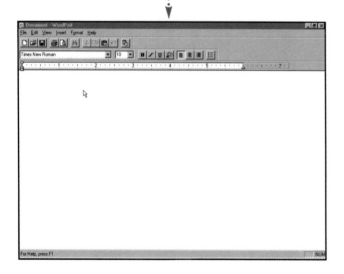

5 WordPad should now be up and running. You are ready for the next step! ■

Learning *<html>*, *<head>*, *<title>*, and *<body>* Tags

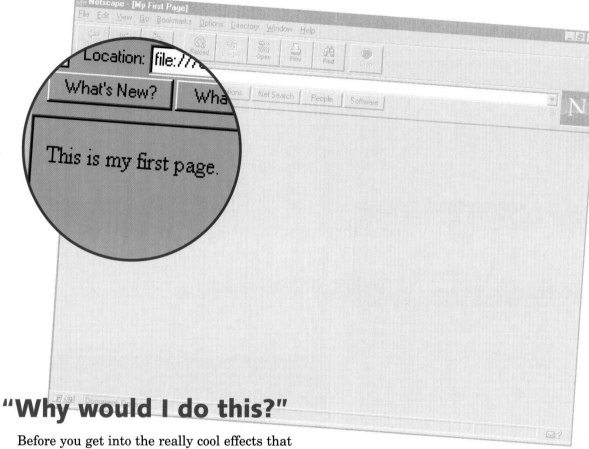

"Why would I do this?"

Before you get into the really cool effects that you can achieve with HTML, you must first learn the basics. These basics include how to start and end a Web page, and giving your page a title. Seem simple? Maybe so, but these tasks are very necessary in the construction of a successful HTML page. Don't worry—you will be performing your own HTML wizardry with advanced tags soon enough!

Task 2: Learning *<html>*, *<head>*, *<title>*, and *<body>* Tags

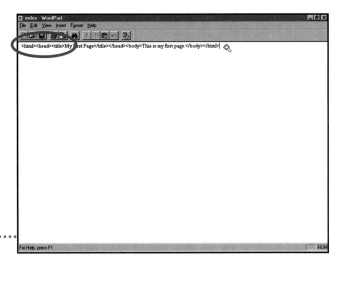

1 At the top of a new page enter the following text:

```
<html><head><title>My First
➡Page</title></head><body>This is
➡my first page.</body></html>
```

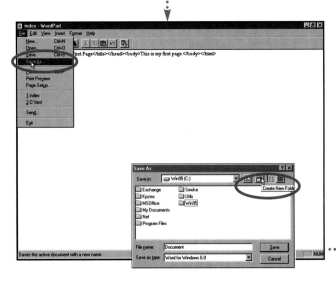

2 Go to the **File** menu and choose **Save As**.

3 Click the **Create New Folder** button.

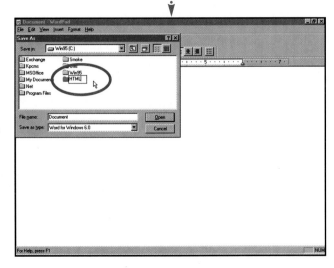

4 Name the folder **HTML** and double-click the new folder. This is where you will store all the files you create while following along with this book.

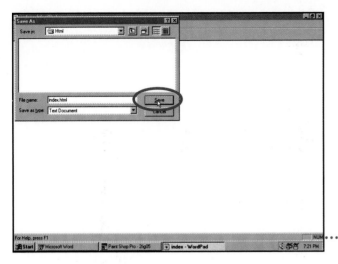

5 Enter the name `index.html` where it says File Name and select **Text Document** as the file type. Then click **Save**.

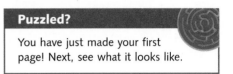

Puzzled?

You have just made your first page! Next, see what it looks like.

6 Now it is time to start your browser. Go to your **Start** menu and start Netscape.

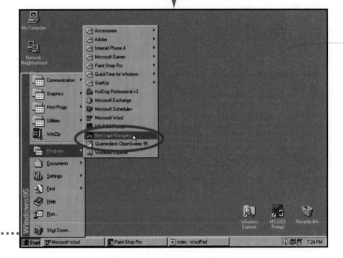

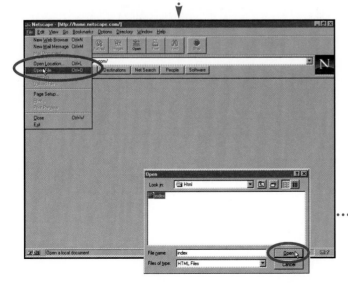

7 Go to the **File** menu and select **Open File**.

8 Change to the HTML directory and select the file titled **index**. Click **Open**.

9 You should now see the page you have created. ■

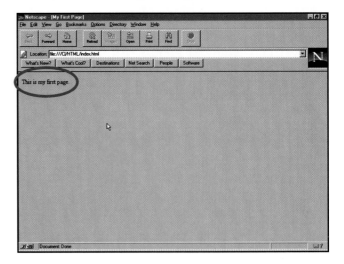

Puzzled?

If you are opening Netscape for the first time, the browser will attempt to connect to the Netscape home page. If you are not connected to an ISP, you will receive an error message.

3

The Header Tags

"Why would I do this?"

The header tags provide a way to produce different sized headings for different uses. For example, the <h1> tag would be used to provide a main heading for your home page and <h2> would be used for a subheading.

Task 3: The Header Tags

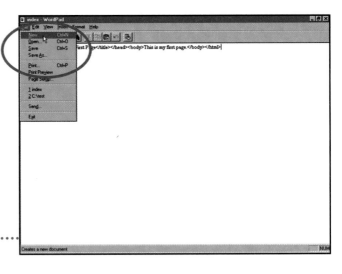

1 Change back to WordPad, go to the **File** menu, and select **New**.

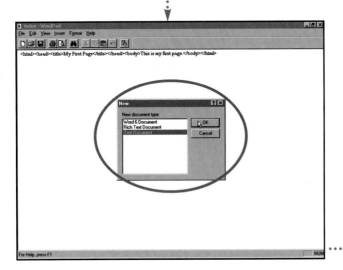

2 When the next menu pops up, select **Text Document** and click the **OK** button.

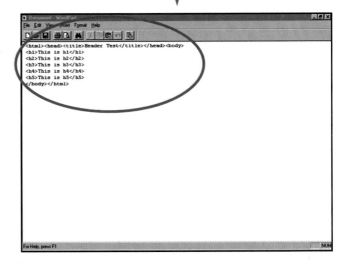

3 Enter the following text and then save the file as **htest.html**:

```
<html><head><title>Header
Test</title></head><body>
<h1>This is h1</h1>
<h2>This is h2</h2>
<h3>This is h3</h3>
<h4>This is h4</h4>
<h5>This is h5</h5>
</body></html>
```

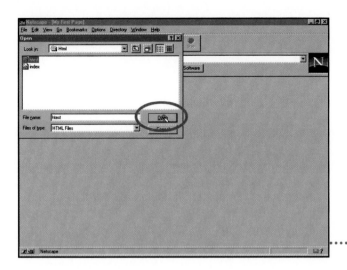

4 Change to Netscape and open the htest.html file.

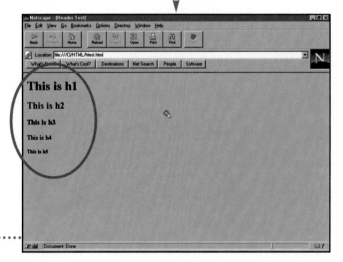

5 As you can see, each header tag has a different effect. The largest heading is <h1> and the smallest is <h5>. Next, you will add a heading to your page!

6 Go back to WordPad and select **Open** in the **File** menu.

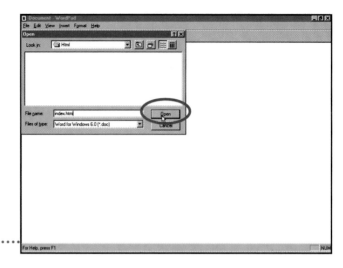

7 Type in **index.html** where it says File Name. This will open the first page on which you have worked.

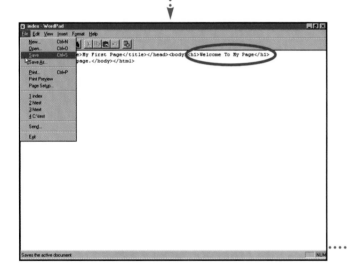

8 Enter the following text directly after the <body> tag and then save the file:

<h1>Welcome To My Page</h1>

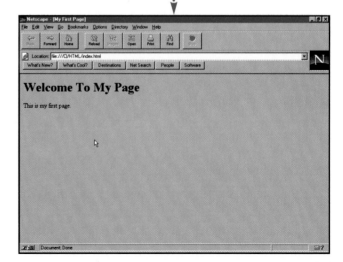

9 Change back to Netscape and open the index.html file. You should see your page with a new title! ■

The *<p>* and *
* Tags

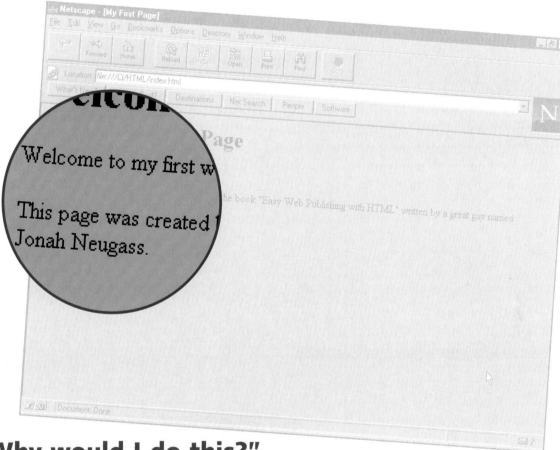

"Why would I do this?"

The <p> and <br> tags are used mainly to create
new paragraphs of text and to separate different elements (such as text and pictures). The

 tag will simply start a new line, while
the <p> tag will skip a line, then start a new
paragraph. Using more than one <p> tag in
sequence has no effect; however, using more
than one <br> tag will skip multiple lines.

Task 4: The *<p>* and *
* Tags

1 You are going to want to change your page slightly to make it more descriptive. Go to WordPad and make sure the index.html file is open; erase the text that says "This is my first page."

2 Enter the following text in place of the sentence that you just deleted:

> Welcome to my first web page!
> ➥This page was created by me with
> ➥help from the book "Easy Web
> ➥Publishing with HTML" written by
> ➥a great guy named Jonah Neugass.

3 Change to Netscape and open the index.html file. You should see the changes you have made.

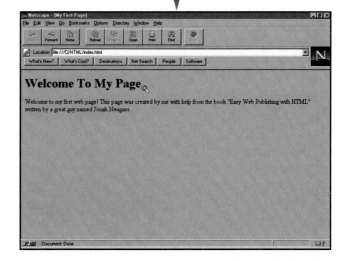

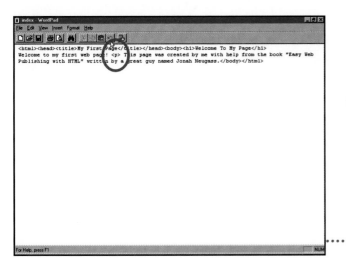

4 Next, you will add a <p> tag to separate some of the text. Change back to WordPad and insert a **<p>** tag after the sentence "Welcome to my first web page!" Save the file.

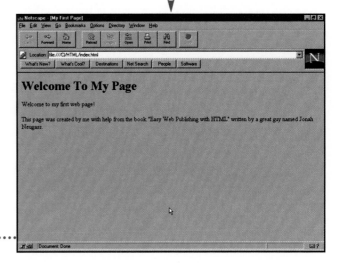

5 Go back to Netscape and open the file index.html. You should see a break between the first and second sentences.

6 OK, on to using the <br> tag. In WordPad, put a <br> tag between the word "named" and the name "Jonah," then save the file.

Task 4: The *<p>* and *
* Tags

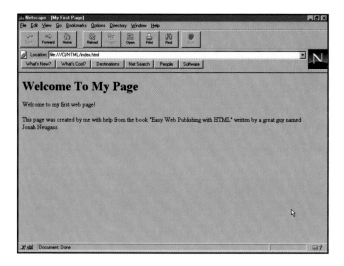

7 If you change back to Netscape and re-load the index.html file, you will notice that the <br> tag forced a break after the word "named". ■

Learning Text Alignment

"Why would I do this?"

In HTML, everything is justified left by default. This means that all the text on a page is aligned on the left side of the page, unless otherwise specified. The <p> tag allows you to change the alignment of text, but first you must add a modifier to that tag. To center a body of text, you use the tag <p align=center> and the </p> tag to end the section to be centered. If you want the text aligned on the right, use <p align=right>, and there you have it!

Task 5: Learning Text Alignment

1 Add the **align=center** to the <p> tag in
WordPad to make it look like this:

<p align=center>

Puzzled?

Another way to center text is to
place the <center></center>
tags around anything you want centered. The <center> tag also lets
you center things such as images
and headings.

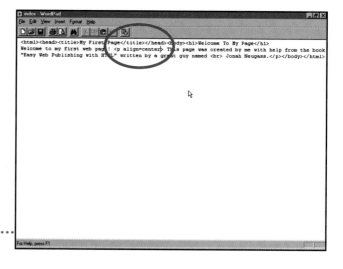

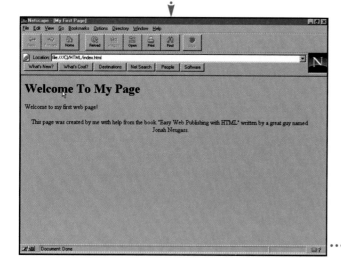

2 Jump to Netscape and open index.html.
You should see the last sentence centered
on the page.

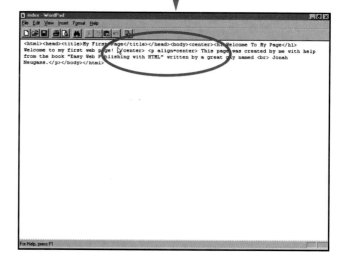

3 You may be thinking that your page looks
a little strange with only part of the text
centered. You can fix that now! Go to
WordPad and insert a <center> tag immediately before the <h1> tag and a </center>
tag immediately before the <p align=
center> tag.

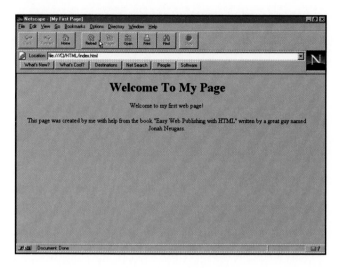

4 Go back to Netscape and reload the index.html file. Congratulations—you can now align text! ■

Changing the Background Color

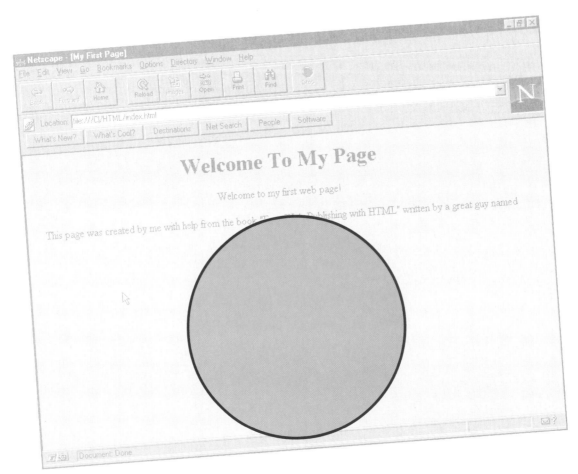

"Why would I do this?"

The default background color for most browsers is gray. Pretty boring, right? Well, in this section you learn how to change your page's background to something a bit more interesting!

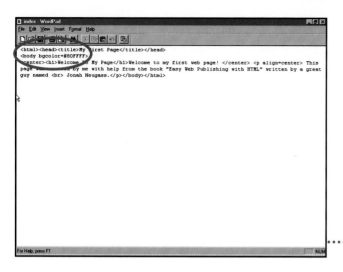

1 Just as you did previously with the <p> tag, you will be modifying the <body> tag to change your page's background color. Change the <body> tag so that it looks like this:

<body bgcolor=#80FFFF>

Save the file.

2 Change to Netscape and load the page. The background color should now be a nice, light blue. ■

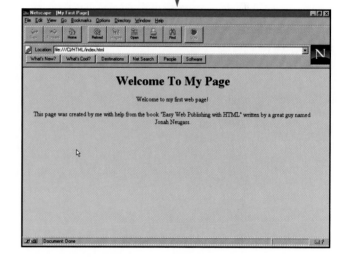

Puzzled?

To modify a color in HTML, you first need its *hexadecimal*, or *hex*, *code*. This code is just a different representative of a set of three colors: red, green, and blue. Because you're not expected to know hexadecimal, a table with a set of standard colors from which you can choose has been included at the end of the book.

Puzzled?

Some color names can be entered directly (red, blue, yellow, green, and the like) without knowing the hex code.

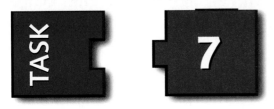

TASK 7

Changing the Text Color

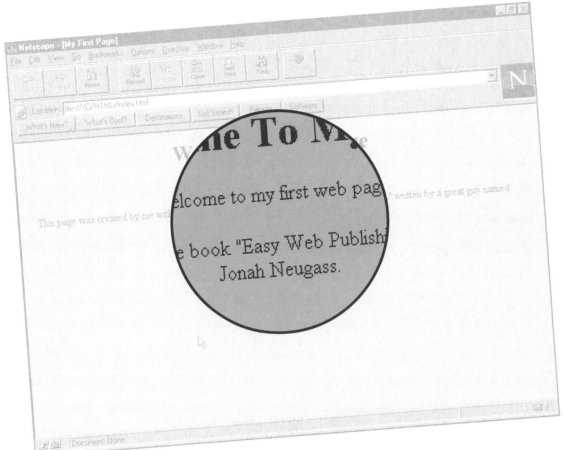

"Why would I do this?"

The reasons for changing the text color are almost exactly the same as the reasons for changing the background color: to spice up your page. One thing you need to watch out for, however, is making your text color and your background too similar; this may make your text unreadable.

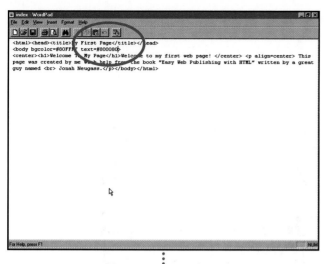

1 Once again, change the <body> tag to look like the following:

```
<body bgcolor=#80FFFF
➥text=#800080>
```

Save the file.

2 Go back to Netscape and reload the page. You should see dark purple text against a light blue background. ■

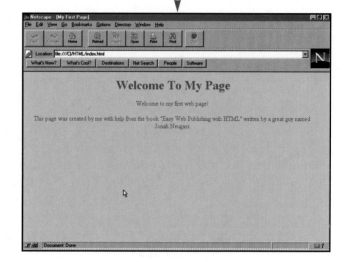

Puzzled?

Changing the text color is almost exactly like modifying the background color. In fact, all you will be doing is adding another modifier to the <body> tag! To create some contrast so that you can read your text, you will pick a great dark purple.

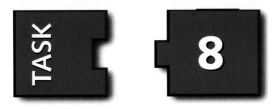

Separating Text with the *<hr>* Tag

"Why would I do this?"

The <hr> tag creates a horizontal line on a page. It is often used to separate a header from a body of text, or even different paragraphs from each other. You will be using it to divide your header, "Welcome To My Page," from the rest of the page.

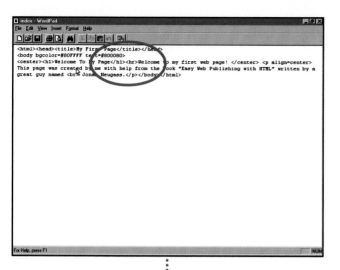

1 Using the <hr> tag is simple. Just put the tag where you want the line to be placed. In this case, put it after the </h1> tag and save the page.

2 As you can see, when you reload the index.html file, you have a nice line that gives your page a bit more definition. ■

Puzzled?

You can add a width modifier to the <hr> tag if you do not want the line to go all the way across the page. For example, if you only wanted the line to go across half the page, you would modify the <hr> tag to look like this:

    <hr width=50%>

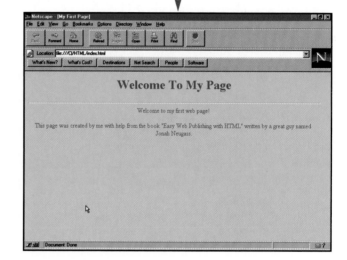

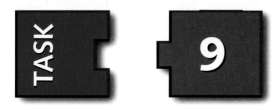

Emphasizing Text with **<b>** and **<i>** Tags

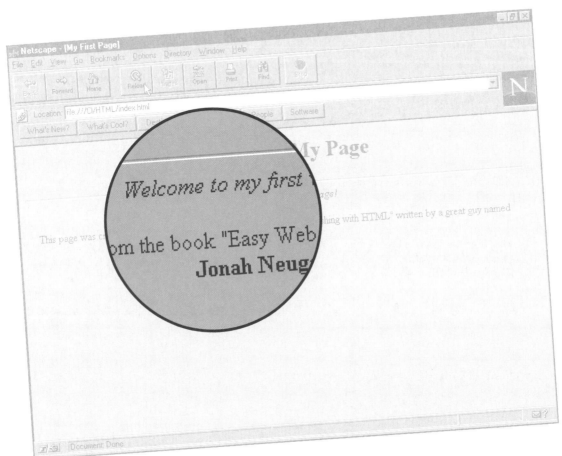

"Why would I do this?"

The <b> and <i> tags give you a way of drawing attention to a certain area of text. If you put <b></b> around a word or a sentence, your text will become bold. If you do the same thing with the <i> tag, your text will be italicized.

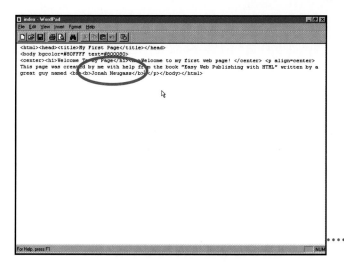

1 Let's start by making the name "Jonah Neugass" bold. To do this, place the <b></b> tags around the name so that it looks like this:

<b>Jonah Neugass<b>

Now, save the page and change to Netscape.

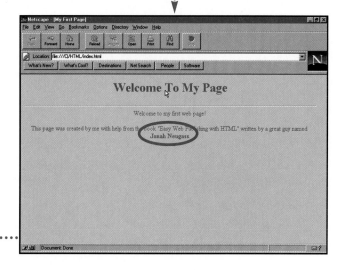

2 Reload the index.html file—the name is in bold text. Now, on to the <i> tag!

3 Now go back to WordPad and place the <i> tags around your first sentence ("Welcome to my first web page!"). You know the routine: save the file and switch to Netscape.

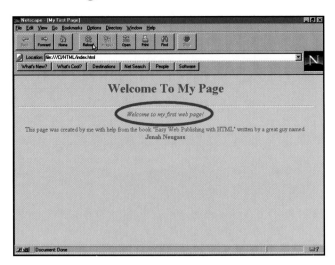

4 Once you reload the index.html file you should see the first sentence in italics. ■

PART II

Links and Navigation

OK, SO NOW YOU KNOW HOW to put together a basic Web page. Feel like there is something missing? Well, if so, you are partially right. One of the great things that HTML provides us is the *hyperlink* (or *link*). These links let you connect your pages not only to other local pages that you create, but to just about any page in the world!

To first understand links you need to know about something called a Uniform Resource Locator, or URL. An URL is basically an address that tells you where to find things on the Web. For example, the URL to one of my Web pages that I am working on is:

```
http://www.cse.nau.edu/~jgn/index.html
```

The first part, "http://", lets you know what kind of *server* will be opened by the URL. The "http://" means that a Web page will be accessed. There are several other services that can be opened with an URL. For example, you can also use "ftp://" to open an ftp session to an ftp site or "mailto:," to start up your local mail program.

The next part, "www.cse.nau.edu," specifies the *host* that stores the page you want to access.

After that, the "/~jgn" tells you in what directory the HTML file is located. There can be several HTML files, including graphics, sounds, or even movies, in the same directory.

The last part of this URL informs you of the name of the file you want to access: in this case, "index.html." This is the standard name for the "main" part of most home pages. In fact, if you leave out the file name, many servers automatically assume you want the index.html file.

Part I taught you how to open the necessary programs for editing and viewing your Web page, in addition to introducing you to the fundamental tags that provide the basis for most HTML files. The second part of this book will teach you how to add links to your pages. There are two main types of links: *relative* and *absolute*. Relative links give you the name of the file you want to access in relation to the page you are on. For example, to access a page called "nextpage.html," which is in the same directory as the index.html file, you would use the following syntax:

```
<a href="nextpage.html">nextpage.html</a>
```

Notice that you don't need to use all that "http://" stuff.

Absolute links are slightly different. They use the entire URL to specify where the next page is to be found. Here is an example of an absolute URL to the nextpage.html file:

```
<a href="http://www.cse.nau.edu/~jgn/
nextpage.html">nextpage.html</a>
```

Now, I know what you are thinking: OK, I understand the difference between relative and absolute links, but what is the stuff you put after the link? The text following the close bracket of the `<a href>` tag is what actually shows up as the link on your Web page. In this case, nextpage.html will show up as a blue link and if you click it, you would go to the actual nextpage file. As for the `</a>`, it is just a *terminator* for the link (it ends the link).

Make sure not to forget this, or everything following your `<a href>` tag will become one big link!

Ok, now you know what links are—let's add some to your page!

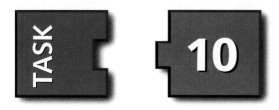

Adding Relative Links

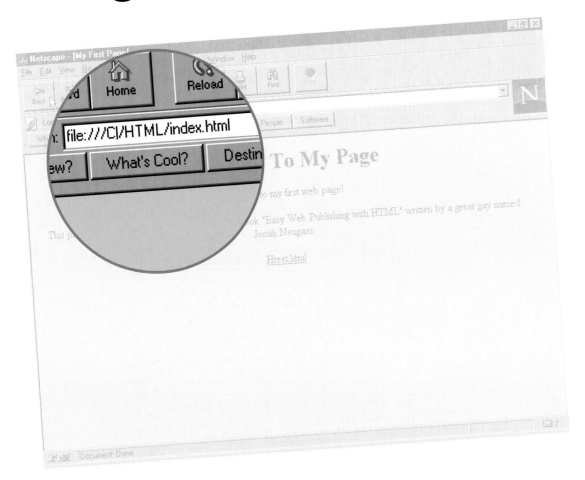

"Why would I do this?"

Again, relative links give a Web author a simple way to link items on the same server. Also, if you move your page to another server, you shouldn't have to change any of your relative links.

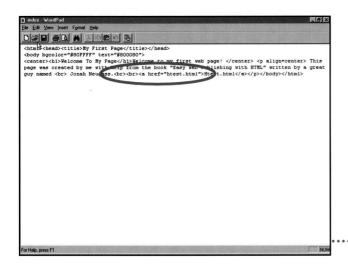

1 Because you really have only worked on two pages, you will add a relative link to your header test page. In WordPad, add the following right before the </p> tag:

```
<br><br><a href="htest.html">
➥Htest.html</a>
```

Save the file.

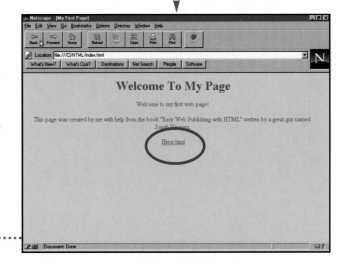

2 Jump to Netscape and load the index.html file. As you can see, your new link has now appeared at the bottom of your area of text.

3 Click on the link to make sure it works. If you did it correctly, you should see your test page! ■

Puzzled?

If for some reason you don't see your test page, go back to WordPad and make sure you have saved the file, then make sure the correct file is loaded in Netscape.

35

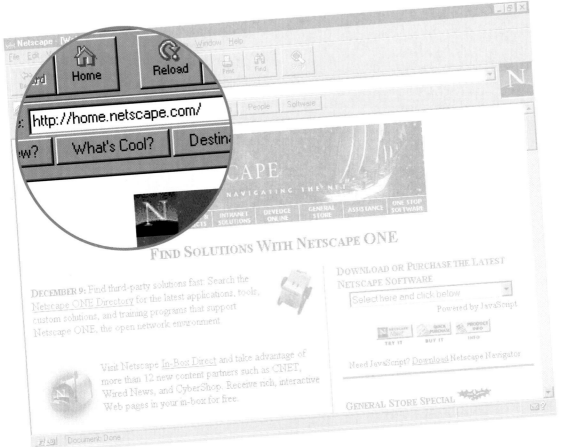

Adding Absolute Links

"Why would I do this?"

Relative links are great for piecing together a series of pages on your own server, but to access the outside world, you need to use absolute links.

1 Add a link from your page to Netscape's. To do this you will need the URL, which is **http://home.netscape.com**. You insert this link after the relative link you added to your test page. The tag should look like this:

```
<br><a href="http://home.netscape
➥.com/">Netscape</a>
```

Missing Link

When you are putting an absolute link on your page, make sure that you copy the URL exactly. If the URL is off by even one letter, your link will not work.

2 Now, save the page and change to Netscape. Once you reload the index.html file, you should see a link to Netscape under your htest.html link.

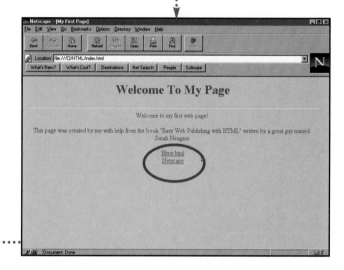

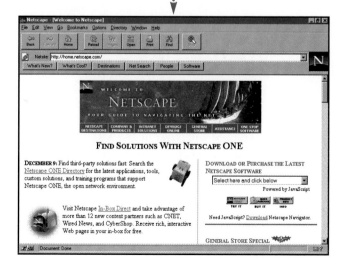

3 Again, you want to test your new link to make sure it works. Click the Netscape link and you should see the Netscape home page appear! ■

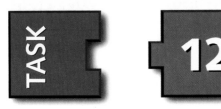

TASK 12

Changing the Link Color

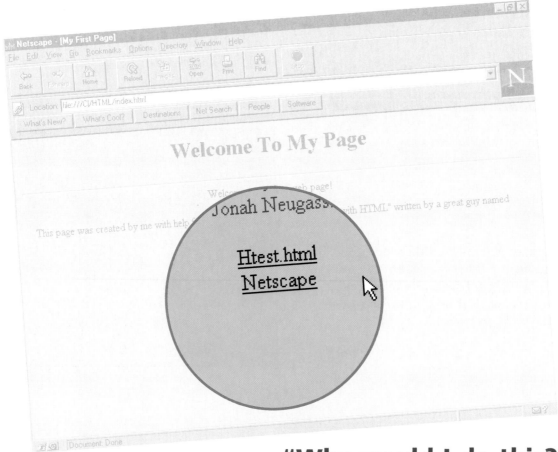

"Why would I do this?"

You may have noticed that the color of your links is very close to the color of the regular text. This can make them hard to distinguish. Solution: change the color of the links! To change the link's color, you must add more modifiers to the <body> tag.

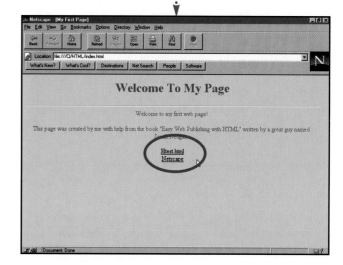

1 To provide some contrast from the background and text, try making your unvisited links red and your visited links black. Change the <body> tag to look like the following:

```
<body bgcolor="#80FFFF" text=
➥"#800080"link="#FF0000" vlink="#000000">
```

The link controls the unvisited link and vlink controls the visited links!

2 As always, save the file and return to Netscape to view the results of your work. Both links have been visited, so both should now be black. ■

Puzzled?

When changing link color, you can change both the *visited* link (links you have been to before) color and the *unvisited* link (links you haven't been to before) color.

PART III

Adding Graphics to Your Pages

GRAPHICS ARE A MAJOR PART OF WHAT make up the World Wide Web (WWW) today. They come in many sizes, colors, and formats and their use can add new interest to what may have previously been a plain, boring page.

There are two standard graphic file formats that most browsers support: GIF and JPG (pronounced Jiff and J-Peg). The GIF picture files currently make up the majority of picture files on the Web. They were one of the first graphic file formats to be incorporated into the WWW and they quickly became the standard for graphics on the Web. They do have

limitations, however. The major problem with GIF files is that they only support 256 different colors. If you have a file you wish to convert into a GIF, you may lose colors or the picture could become *dithered*. Dithering refers to when the program tries to find the best 256 colors for the image file, which may have previously been up to 16 million colors. Needless to say, the results of dithering are sometimes unpleasant. The second major problem with GIF files is that they can become quite large. Large picture files are a problem on the WWW because many users connect to the Internet over slow modem lines. If you have three or four large files that each take four minutes to download, nobody would want to take the time to look at your page.

The JPG file format takes steps to solve some of the problems users experience with GIF files. JPG files are not limited to 256 colors, but allow up to 16 million colors. This may seem excessive, but the maximum number of colors is rarely used. The second improvement that JPG files have incorporated is compression. JPG files use a *lossy* compression scheme to make their files smaller. Lossy is the quality of the picture, which depends on how much compression is involved. However, some of the older browsers do not support JPG files.

As a general rule, when adding graphics to your Web pages, try to keep them under 10K bytes—nothing over 30K—as it can take a long time for the average Web surfer (on a 28.8 modem) to load. Also, because graphics are so exciting, you may want to include every picture file you have ever seen on your page. Resist that urge. Use of graphics can be overdone.

Unfortunately, because this book does not come with a diskette or a CD, you will have to find your own graphics to add to your pages. Luckily, finding pictures on the Web is very easy.

13

Adding Graphics to Your Page

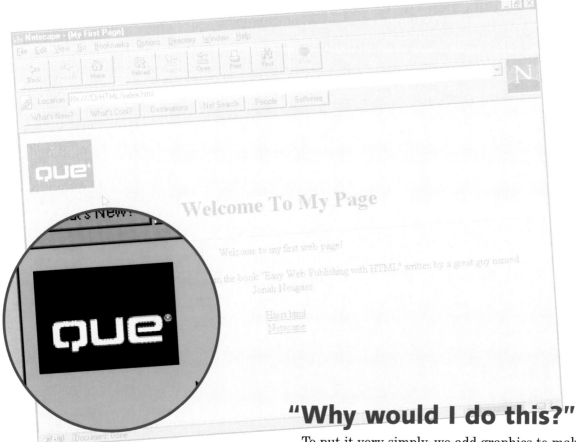

"Why would I do this?"

To put it very simply, we add graphics to make our pages interesting. Remember the cliché "a picture is worth a thousand words?" Well, it can be true! The tag you use to insert a graphic is the <img> tag. You use the tag with an *src modifier*, to tell the browser where the file is located on the server. For a picture called "foo.gif", the completed tag would look like this:

```
<img src="foo.gif">
```

1 You want to insert the que.gif file at the top of the page before the heading. Insert the following tag before the <center> tag and save the file:

```
<img src="que.gif" alt="que.gif">
```

Puzzled?

The image, que.gif, is a file I created for demonstration purposes. The src modifier is used to define a link to the picture file. You can use relative or absolute links with src.

Puzzled?

You added the alt modifier above so that if the person does not display images in his or her browser, then que.gif would be displayed in its place.

2 When you switch to Netscape and load the index.html file, you should see the new graphic in the upper left-hand corner. ■

Missing Link

You can also use an absolute URL in the source tag to represent the picture file's location.

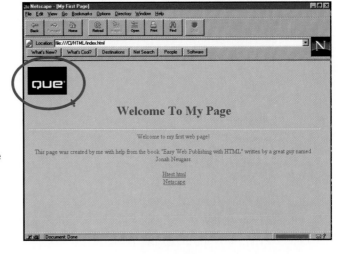

Aligning Graphics

"Why would I do this?"

Sometimes when you add a graphic, it is not
exactly where you want it in relation to your
text. By default, a page break is inserted after
the <img> tag. You can change this by adding an
align modifier. This enables you to align your
graphic to the left, right, middle, top, or bottom
of the next line of text. The <center> tag will
also work on images.

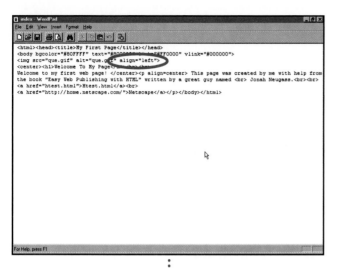

1 You want to align your graphic on the left side of your header. In order to do this, add the align modifier to your <img> tag so that it looks like this:

```
<img src="que.gif" alt="que.
➥gif" align="left">
```

You also want to add a <br> tag after the </h1> tag so the <hr> tag won't be on the same line as your image.

2 After you have saved the file, jump to Netscape and reload the index.html file. Your image is now aligned with your heading. Also, you may want to go ahead and try "right" or "center" in the above command to get a feel for how this command can easily move your images. Remember, if you don't like the effect, you can always change it back! ■

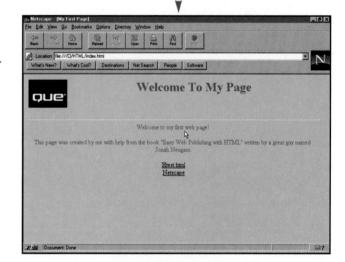

Puzzled?

You may notice that the heading seems to be shifted to the right. This is because of the <center> tag. If the <center> tag was not present, the heading would be flush against the right side of the image.

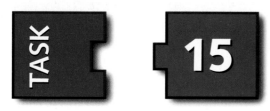
Using Graphics as Links

"Why would I do this?"

Graphics for decoration are great, but they can also be combined with links to make—you guessed it—*graphical links*. Graphical links are often used on Web pages and buttons. For example, a forward or backward arrow can be used to move through a series of sequential pages. Making a graphical link is easy: All you do is add an `<a href></a>` around your `<img>` tag.

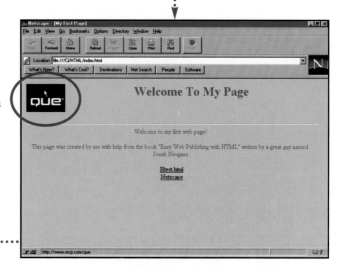

1 Because you have the Que logo on your page, you might as well make it a link to the Que home page! To do this, add an `<a href>` tag around the graphic so that it looks like this:.

```
<a href="http://www.mcp.
➥com/que"><img src="que.
➥gif" alt="que.gif" align ="left"
➥border=0></a>
```

If you look at the `<img>` tag, you will notice that you added a border modifier. Since you don't want a border this time, set the tag equal to zero.

2 Jump back to Netscape. When you position your cursor over the Que graphic, you should notice an URL appear on the bottom left corner of your browser (denoting a link).

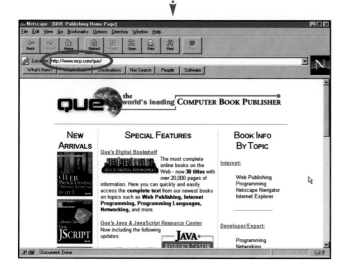

3 Click the link to make sure it works. You should see Que's Web page appear! ∎

Inserting a Background Picture

"Why would I do this?"

Background pictures (for example, the blue pattern shown in the above figure) can be used for several reasons. For instance, they can serve a special purpose that doesn't come across with just plain background (a company logo, for instance). They can also be used simply because they are neat. Some rules I try to follow:

- Make sure the picture isn't too big (keep it under 30K).

- Don't make it too garish or noisy, as that detracts from the rest of the page.

- If a graphic is too small to fill the entire browser window, the image may repeat, causing *tiling*. Make sure if you use a background picture or pattern that it tiles well, meaning that it looks okay if the image is aligned side by side with itself.

1 To add a background picture to your page, you must add a modifier to the <body> tag. Since you don't need the bgcolor modifier, you will remove it and replace it with the background modifier, so that it looks like this:

```
<body background="background.
➥jpg" text="#800080" link
➥="#FF0000" vlink="#000000">
```

2 After you save the file, go to Netscape and reload the index.html file. The page will have a new background image. Notice that while the image repeats itself, there are no clashing edges where each picture meets. ■

PART IV

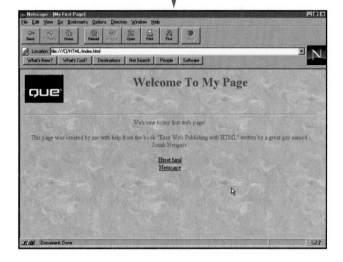

Organizing Pages with Lists

PEOPLE USE LISTS for a great many things. There are shopping lists, lists of things to do, and lists of phone numbers and addresses. Lists are useful because they give you a way to put your ideas into an organized form.

HTML supports three main types of lists: numbered, bulleted, and definition lists. Each has its own advantages. For example, numbered lists are great for describing sequential tasks or anything that follows a step-by-step procedure. Bulleted lists are mainly used for drawing attention to important points (in no particular order). Finally, definition lists are good for lists that necessitate descriptions for each list item.

There are several tags you need to know in order to create these lists. To start and end a numbered list, use the <ol></ol> tags (the "ol" stands for ordered list). For bulleted lists, use <ul></ul> (you guessed it, unordered list). Finally, for definition lists, use <dl></dl> (for definition list).

Once you have given the start and end tags for your list, you have to actually insert items into the list. Numbered and bulleted lists insert items in the same way. To insert a list heading, use the tags <lh></lh>, and for regular items, use <li></li>. For a definition list, you must use <dd> for a heading and <dt> for its definition.

In this part, you see an example of what each list looks like and how to insert each into your own home page!

Creating a Bulleted List

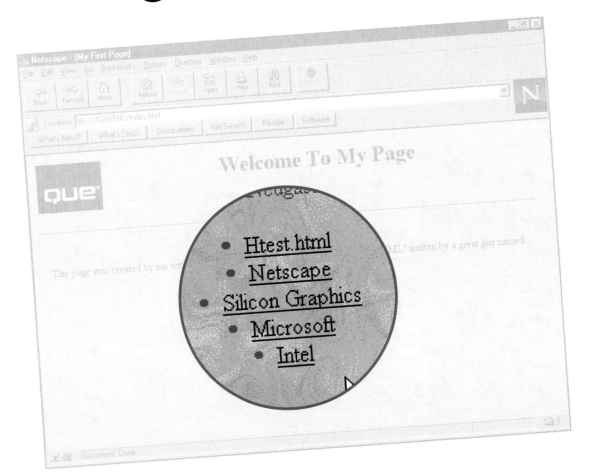

"Why would I do this?"

Bulleted lists are used mainly for bringing attention to certain important items on a page. Here, you use a bulleted list to bring attention to your links.

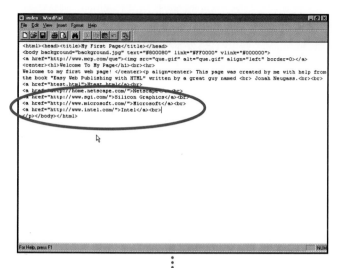

1 First, add a few links to fill out your list a bit better. Add the following under your link to Netscape:

```
<a href="http://www.sgi.com/
➥">Silicon Graphics</a><br>

<a href="http://www.microsoft.com/
➥">Microsoft</a><br>

<a href="http://www.intel.com/
➥">Intel</a><br>
```

2 Save the file as **index.html** and go to Netscape. You should see your new links. Now add your list. Put the **<ul>** before the link to your test page. Surround each link with the <li></li> pair. Finally, put the **</ul>** tag after the the last </li> tag to end the list. Your final product should look like the following bold text:

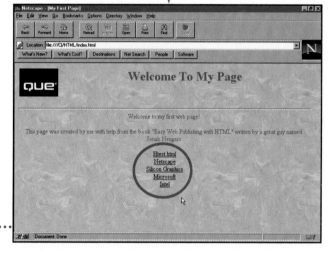

3
```
<ul>
<li><a hef="htest.html">Htest.html</
➥a><br></li>
<li><a href="http://home.netscape
➥.com/">Netscape</a><br></li>
<li><a href="http://www.sgi.com/
➥">Silicon Graphics</a><br></li>
<li><a href="http://www.microsoft
➥.com/">Microsoft</a><br></li>
<li><a href="http://www.intel.com/
➥">Intel</a><br></li>
</ul>
```

Save the file.

4 When you reload the index file in Netscape, you will notice that the list is not affected by the `<p align="center">`. You should fix that now. Also, you may want to remove the `<br>` tags after each list item, as a line break is automatically inserted after the end of each list item. Your modified list will look like the following bold text:

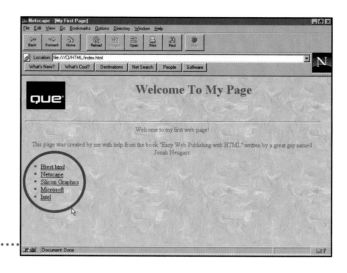

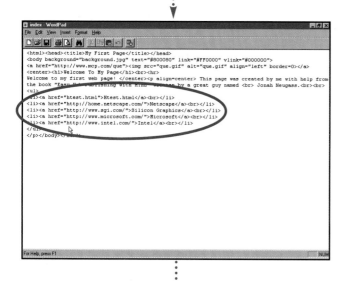

5
```
<center><ul>
<li><a href="htest.html">Htest.html
➥</a></li>
<li><a href="http://home.netscape.
➥com/">Netscape</a></li>
<li><a href="http://www.sgi.
➥com/">Silicon Graphics</a></li>
<li><a href="http://www.microsoft.
➥com/">Microsoft</a></li>
<li><a href="http://www.intel.com/
➥">Intel</a></li>
</ul></center>
```

6 Again, save the file and reload it in Netscape. You will see your bulleted list centered on the page (it may look a little funny right now, but you will take care of it a few tasks down the road). ■

Creating a Numbered List

"Why would I do this?"

Numbered lists are good for organizing items
that have sequential properties. For example,
this book can be thought of as one big, numbered list: each task has a number, and you
must follow them in order to get the same Web
pages that appear at the end of the lessons.

Task 18: Creating a Numbered List

1 Let's make another test page. Open a new document in WordPad and add the following:

```
<html><head><title>Numbered List
➡Test</title></head>
<body>
<ol>
<lh>My shopping list for this
➡week:</lh>
<li>Milk</li>
<li>Butter</li>
<li>Eggs</li>
<li>Onions</li>
<li>Chicken</li>
</ol>
```

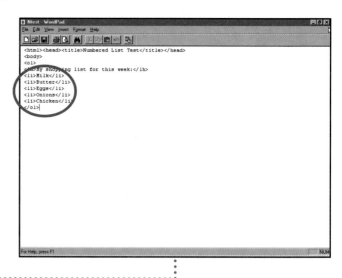

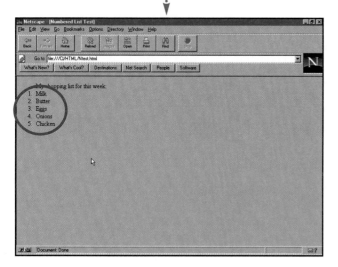

Missing Link

Numbered lists will handle the incrementing of each item, but will also take care of the spacing between the number and the listed item. For example, if you later decide you want to insert another item into your list, all of the list entries would automatically be renumbered in the correct order.

2 After you have saved the file as **Ntest.html**, change to Netscape, load the new file Ntest.html, and you will see your new numbered list! ■

TASK 19

Creating a Definition List

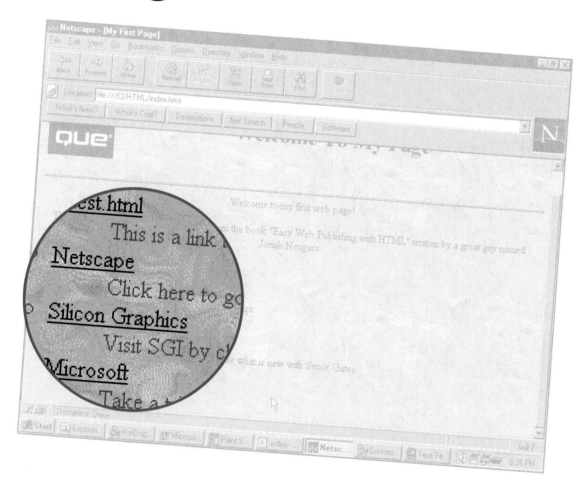

"Why would I do this?"

The last type of list is the definition list. Definition lists can be thought of as entries in a dictionary—you first have the statement of the word, which is then followed by the word's definition. These lists can be used the same way.

Task 19: Creating a Definition List

1 One of the great things about HTML is that it lets you *nest* tags, which means you can have more than one tag inside another. You will use this feature to create a definition list with your bulleted list of links for your headings. Open the index.html file in Wordpad and change your list so it looks like the bold text below:

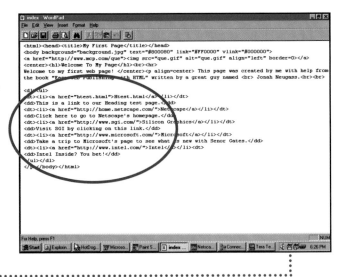

Puzzled?

You removed the
 tags that you
had added two parts ago in order to
see the full result of the definition lists.

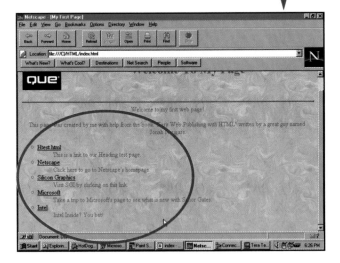

```
<dl><ul>
<dt><li><a href="htest
➥.html">Htest.html</a></li></dt>
<dd>This is a link to our Heading
➥test page./dd>
<dt><li><a href="http://home
➥.netscape.com/">Netscape</a>
➥</li></dt>
<dd>Click here to go to
➥Netscape's homepage./dd>
<dt><li><a href="http://www.sgi
➥.com/">Silicon
➥Graphics</a></li></dt>
<dd>Visit SGI by clicking on this
➥link./dd>
<dt><li><ahref="http://www
➥.microsoft.com/">Microsoft</a>
➥</li></dt>
<dd>Take a trip to Microsoft's
➥page to see what is new with
➥Senor Gates.</dd>
<dt><li><ahref="http://www
➥.intel.com/">Intel</a></li><dt>
<dd>Intel Inside? You bet!</dd>
```

2 After you have saved the file, jump to Netscape and load the index.html file. As you can see, the definition list has done several things for your text including indentation of the "definition text" and retention of the bullet on each hyperlink section. ■

PART V

Organizing Pages with Tables

ANOTHER ONE OF THE FEATURES that HTML provides for data organization is use of tables. HTML tables let you reproduce tables found in spreadsheet programs such as Microsoft Excel and can also be used to align images and text. Some of the best examples of tables on the Web that I have seen are product listings. The manufacturer will use one column for the product name, one for the price, and another for an item description.

Another example of table use is for aligning items on a page to give it the feel of a newspaper layout. This is often hard to do because of HTML's lack of text formatting features, but by making the table border invisible and separating text into different columns, you can give a page that professional "printed" feel.

Here are the tags you need to know to create a table:

`<table>`	The basis for the table; modifiers include border, width, height, cell padding, and cell spacing; terminated with `</table>`
`<tr>`	Constitutes a table row; terminated with `</tr>`
`<th>`	Denotes a table heading; terminated with `</th>`
`<td>`	Signifies a table column; terminated with `</td>`
`<caption>`	Creates a table caption; terminated with `</caption>`

Let's build your first table now!

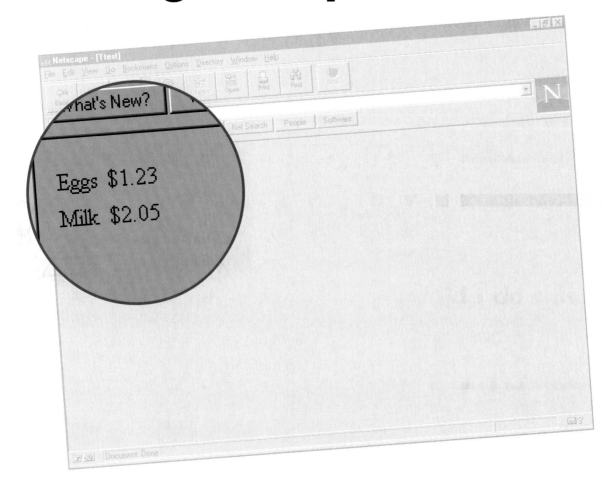

Creating a Simple Table

"Why would I do this?"

I start off small to show you the basics of creating tables. In this task, you create a 2×2 table with no frills.

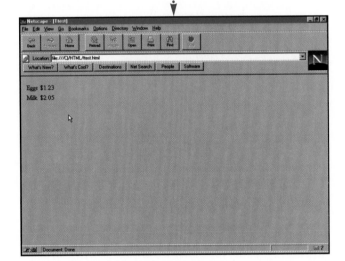

1 Create a file in which to test your table. Start a new file in WordPad. Next, add the <table></table> tags and two <tr></tr> and <td></td> tags to get a 2×2 table. Enter the following code:

```
<html><head><title>Ttest</title></head>
<body>
<table
<tr><td>Eggs</td><td>$1.23</td></tr>
<tr><td>Milk</td><td>$2.05</td></tr>
</table>
</body>
</html>
```

2 Save the file as Ttest.html and load the file in Netscape. If you notice, there is no border separating the entries from one another. You will take care of that next! ■

Adding a Border to Your Table

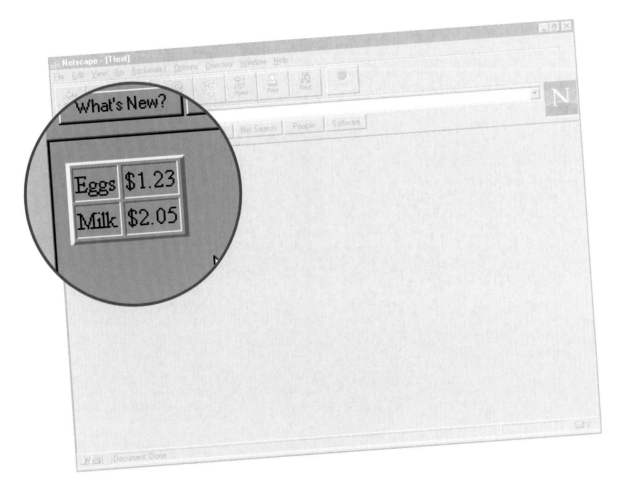

"Why would I do this?"

Most people add borders to give their table a sense of definition, or just to make it look more like a table. That is what you will do now.

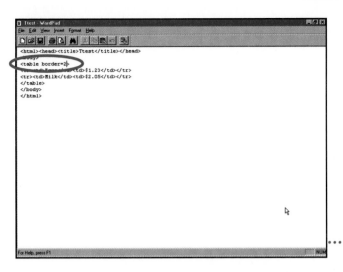

1 Adding a border is easy—just change the `<table>` tag to look like this:

`<table border=2>`

It's done! Pretty simple, right? You have just given your table a two-*pixel* border.

Puzzled?

What you see on your computer screen is essentially made up of very small square units called pixels. By using `<table border=2>` you are telling the browser that you want the border around the table to be two-pixels wide. Note that you use that particular size because it is not too big or too small for these purposes.

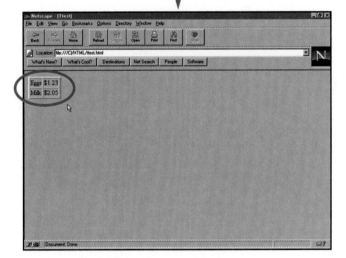

2 Save the file after you are done making the changes above and then switch to Netscape. When you reload the Ttest.html file you will see the border around your table. ■

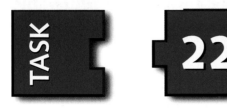

Changing Table Heights and Widths

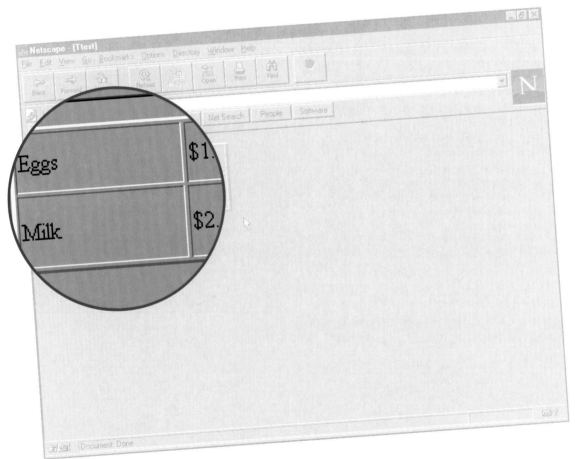

"Why would I do this?"

Being able to change the table height and width can be very important. Did you notice how, in the previous exercise, the data seemed cramped into the very small table cells? Well, you will change that now.

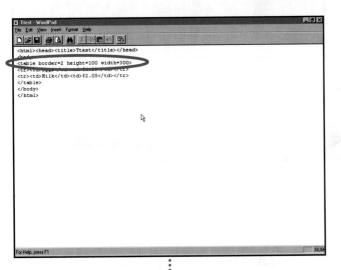

1 To change the table height and width, you must add two more modifiers to the `<table>` tag, those being **height** and **width**. You should make these **100** and **300** pixels respectively. Here is what the `<table>` tag should look like after modification:

```
<table border=2 height=100width=300>
```

2 Save the file after you are done making the changes above and then switch to Netscape. You will see that your table has grown in both height and width when you reload the Ttest.html file. ■

> **Puzzled?**
>
> Every table is broken down into cells. A cell is an area that has a distinct column and row number.

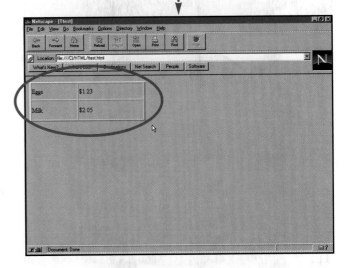

Adding a Caption

"Why would I do this?"

There is one very simple reason to add a caption to a table: to tell someone what the table means. To add a caption, you have to use the <caption></caption> tags. The caption usually comes after the <table> tag.

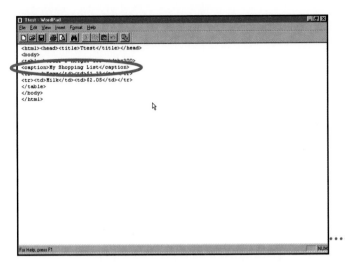

1 Now add the caption **My Shopping List** to the table. Insert the following tag after the `<table>` declaration and save the file:

```
<caption>My Shopping List</
➥caption>
```

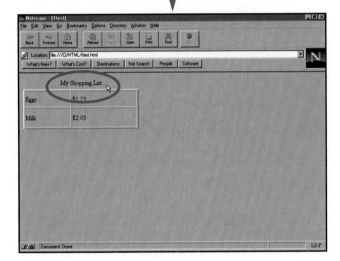

2 In Netscape, reload the Ttable.html. As you can see, your caption is centered over your table! ■

Changing Cell Spacing and Padding

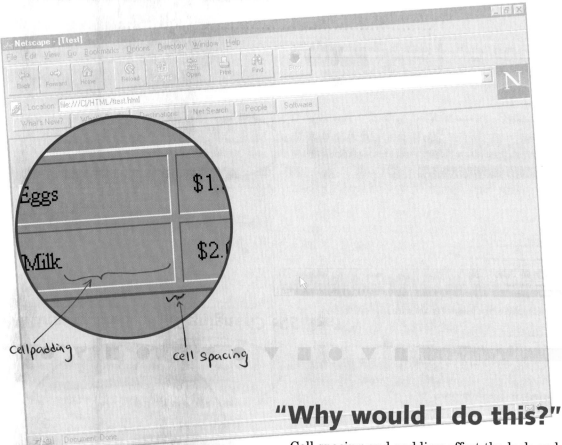

cellpadding

cell spacing

"Why would I do this?"

Cell spacing and padding affect the look and feel of a table. Both of these effects can be added with modifiers to the <table> tag. Cell spacing determines the distance between the outside edge of a cell and the outside border; cell padding determines how far from the left inside edge the items inside the cells are padded. The modifiers for the <table> tag you use are cellspacing and cellpadding.

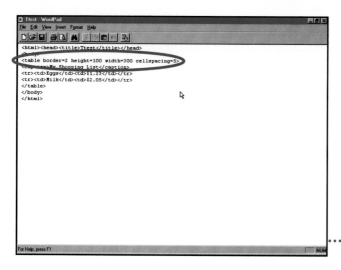

1 You now add the `cellspacing` modifier to the `<table>` tag with a value of five. This means that there will be five pixels' distance between the border and the edge of the cell. Here is what the tag should look like after your modification:

```
<table border=2 height=100 width
➥=300 cellspacing=5>
```

Save the file and jump to Netscape.

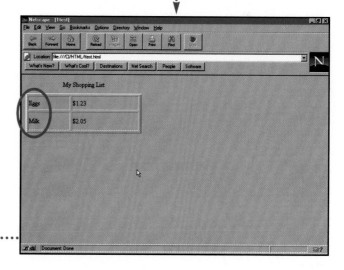

2 Time to reload your file and see what has happened to your table. Can you see the difference?

3 Now, let's use the `cellpadding` modifier to create some space between your text and the edge of the cell. Change the `<table>` tag so that you have a pad of **10** pixels. The finished tag should look like this:

```
<table border=2 height=100 width
➥=300 cellspacing=5 cellxpadding
➥=10>
```
(one word)

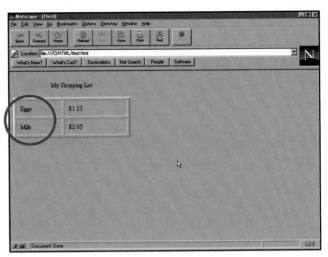

4 Once you have saved the file, change to Netscape and reload Ttext.html so you can see your changes. Notice that your table text is now noticeably farther "into" the cell. ■

Adding Table Headings

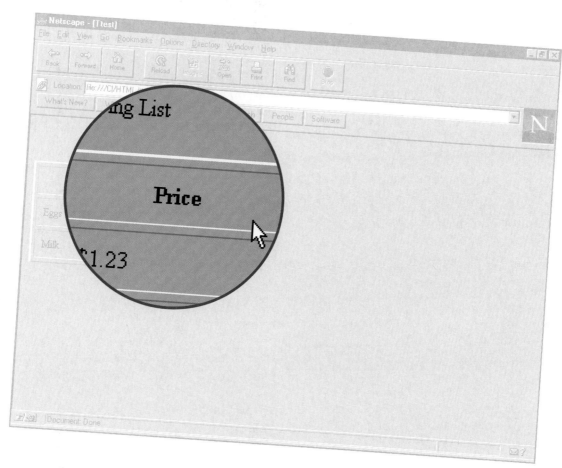

"Why would I do this?"

Okay, so now you have a table. Feel like something is still missing? Well, if so, you are right! Most tables have some sort of heading along the side or top of the table that describes each row and column. These are called *table headings* and you will add them now with the <th></th> tags.

Task 25: Adding Table Headings

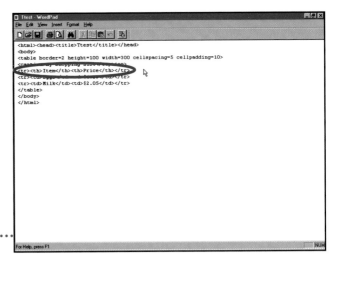

1 To add table headings, you will have to increase the number of rows in your table by one. Add the following line immediately after the caption and save the file:

```
<tr><th>Item</th><th>Price</th></tr>
```

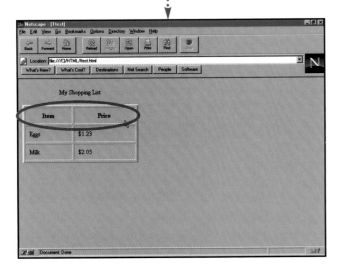

2 Once you reload the file, you will see your new table headings in bold text above your table items. ■

PART VI

Cool Page Layout with Frames

ONE OF THE NEWEST FEATURES to come down the HTML pipeline is the *frame*. Frames enable you to divide a page into several areas, with each area having a different HTML source page.

The release of the first browser that supported frames set thousands of Web developers into a frenzy to get their pages up-to-date with the new technology. Unfortunately, many HTML authors went a little frame-crazy and constructed pages with as many as six to seven different frame areas on one screen! Keep this in mind when building your own pages: don't go overboard. Even though two or three different areas may be cool, too many can be annoying. Remember, you want to draw people to your page, not drive them away.

Here are the frame-related tags covered in this part of the book:

`<frameset>` Defines the number of columns and rows on the page as well as their size; Terminated with `</frameset>`

`<frame>` Tells the browser what HTML file goes in a specific area; Terminated with `</frame>`

`<noframes>` Used for people who may not have browsers that support frames; Terminated with `</noframes>`

Adding a Frame

"Why would I do this?"

Frames are fun and can add a professional look to a page. You can even use frames to load other peoples' pages inside your own. Just remember that too many frames on one page can be confusing or just plain ugly.

1 To use frames, you first have to create two additional HTML files. Open the index.html file in WordPad. Next, highlight all the text up to the </h1> tag and press **CTRL+C** at the same time. This copies the section of highlighted text into memory.

2 You now want to open a new WordPad file and press **CTRL+V** to paste the text into your new file. Add an </html> tag at the end of the file and save it as ~~Header~~.html.
Heading.

> **Missing Link**
>
> If you decide to use frames for your page, it is usually a good idea to also include a <noframes> area so that people with older browsers can still access your page.

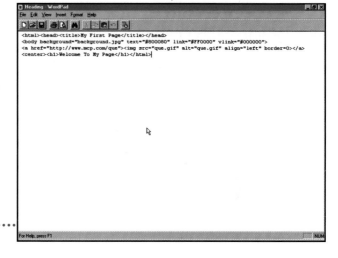

3 To create the HTML file that will occupy your other frame area, go back to your index.html file. Copy all the text from the word "Welcome," all the way down to the </html> tag. Again, press **CTRL+C** to copy the section to memory.

4 Create a new WordPad file and paste the text using **CTRL+V**. Go back to the beginning of the file and add an **<html>** tag, plus your modified body tag:

```
<body background=
➡"background.jpg" text=
➡"#800080" link=
➡"#FF0000" vlink="#000000">
```

Save the file as **Body.html**.

5 Time to add frames! First, use the **<frameset>** tag to tell the browser what size frame. At the beginning of the index.html file, insert the following tag:

```
<frameset rows="100,*">
```

The rows modifier determines how many columns you will have and how large they will be.

Missing Link

When determining frame size, you can use either the pixel size of a window, a percentage of the window you want to use (ie: 50%,50%), or an "*", which will use the rest of the available window area.

6 Next, you have to determine what files will be loaded in each of the rows. Add these two tags after the <frameset> tag:

```
<frame src="Heading.html">
<frame src="Body.html">
```

This will load the Heading.html file in your first row and the Body.html file in your second row.

7 Don't worry, you are almost done. The next step is to add the <noframes> tag so that people with older browsers can see your page. Insert the <noframes> tag after the second <frame> tag.

8 Your last step is to add tags so that you can insert the terminators to the frame tags. At the end of the file, add the **</noframes>** and **</frameset>** tags. Save the file and go to Netscape.

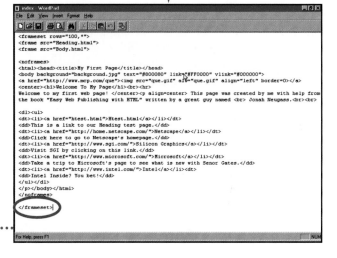

9 Load the index.html file. Congratulations, you have created your first page with frames! ■

Bug?
— Once new linked page is loaded, cannot go back to "index.html" — keeps re-loading the new page!

Modifying Links for Frames

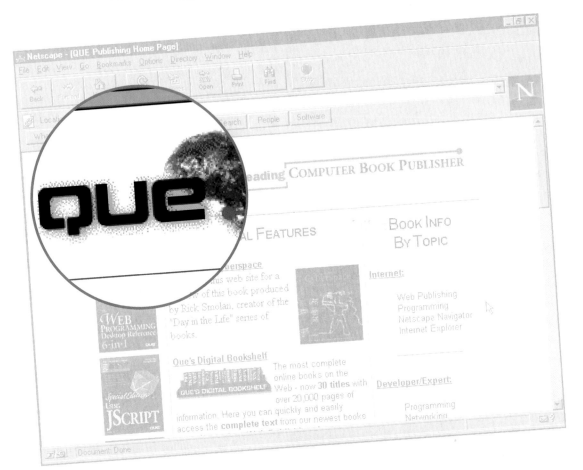

"Why would I do this?"

Currently, if you click a link on your page, the new page will be loaded in its frame area. That can be a problem. For instance, you do not want to load the Que home page in your heading window if you click the Que logo. To change this, you have to alter the links with the target modifier.

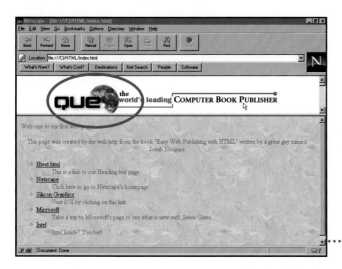

1 Let's start out by seeing what happens when you visit the Que link before your changes. Go to Netscape and click the **Que logo** in the header area.

2 In WordPad, open the Heading.html file. Change the Que home page link to the following and save the file:

```
<a href="http://www.mcp.com/
➥que" target="_top">
```

Target = _self ⟹ Same frame

Target = _top ⟹ Whole page

Target = _blank ⟹ new browser window

Target = _parent ⟹ parent frame

3 Change to Netscape and reload the index.html file. Again, click the **Que logo**. This time, the Que page loads over your own, instead of in the header window. ■

Missing Link

If you add a name=*name* modifier to your `<frame>` tag, you can use a frame area as a target for links in other frames. For example, if I had named the body area "body", I could have altered the Que page to appear in the body area instead.

how do → you name frame areas?

TASK 28

Resizing a Frame

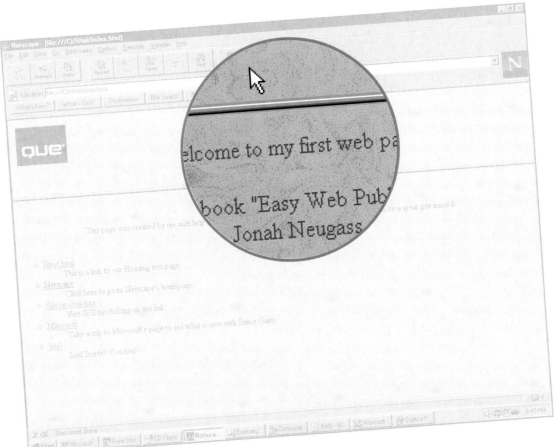

"Why would I do this?"

Resizing a frame can be an essential part of
making your page look professional. Imagine—
you have created your frames and inserted all
your text and graphics, but one of your picture
files is cut in half by one of the frame borders.
There are two ways to solve this problem if you
want to keep the picture where it is: resize the
graphic or resize the frame.

1 Load the index.html file and alter the **<frameset>** tag to enlarge your first row. Change the **<frameset>** tag to the following:

```
<frameset rows="150,*">
```

This will increase the size of your first row by 50 pixels.

doesn't work in Communicator 4.5!

instead, can dynamically change the width of frame in browser window!

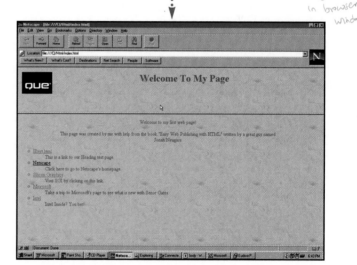

2 Next, change to Netscape and reload the index.html file. You should see your page with the new, resized frame. ■

PART VII

Creating an Imagemap

IMAGEMAPS HAVE BECOME very popular within the last year or so. Many people use them for menus, others, to navigate geographical maps. However they are used, imagemaps can add flair to any page. Think your site is boring? Replace those old text links with a spiffy imagemap.

An imagemap is made up of two parts: the imagemap code and the graphic that accesses that code. The code is made up of a series of active areas that are associated with certain coordinates of the image. A link is also related with each area. When a certain area is clicked, the browser jumps to the associated link.

One of the major uses of imagemaps is to provide a graphical *button bar*. For example, say you have a graphic with three different buttons: one for a guestbook, one for a link page, and one for a test page. An active area would be made for each button and corresponding links would be assigned to those areas. When visitors to your page want to access your list of links, all they have to do is click your imagemap's links button!

Downloading an Imagemap Program

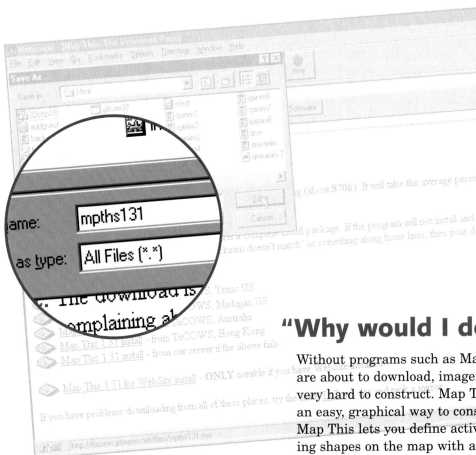

"Why would I do this?"

Without programs such as Map This, which you are about to download, imagemaps would be very hard to construct. Map This gives the user an easy, graphical way to construct imagemaps. Map This lets you define active areas by drawing shapes on the map with an easy-to-use tool. You can also determine to where the area links by double-clicking it and entering the appropriate URL. Without programs such as this, imagemaps would definitely not be as popular as they are. Imagine trying to figure out the coordinates of every specific area by hand. It's not a pleasant thought. In this part, you learn not only where to download Map This, but how it's used, as well.

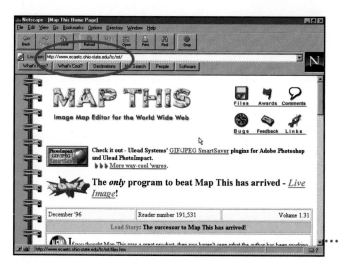

1 Change to Netscape and load **http://www.ecaetc.ohiostate.edu/tc/mt/**. This will take you to the Map This home page, where you can download the software.

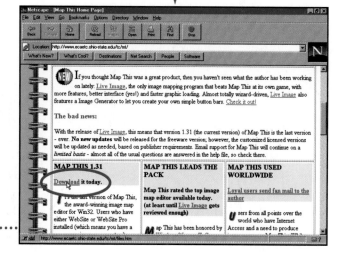

2 Scroll down the page until you find the download link for Map This and click it.

3 On the next page, select the download site closest to you and click it.

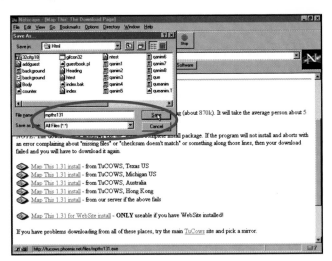

4 When the Save As menu appears, save the file in your HTML directory. The next lesson shows you how to use Map This now that you have it downloaded. ■

Adding Active Areas to an Imagemap

"Why would I do this?"

Active areas on an imagemap determine what is *hot*, or what areas, when clicked, will act as links to different URLs. This is very important, because without them, all parts of the imagemap would connect to the same spot, thus acting as one big link.

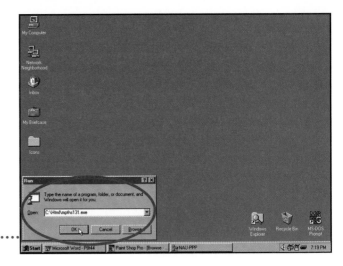

1 To continue the imagemap process, you must first install Map This. From the **Start** menu, select **Run** and enter **C:\Html\mpths131.exe**.

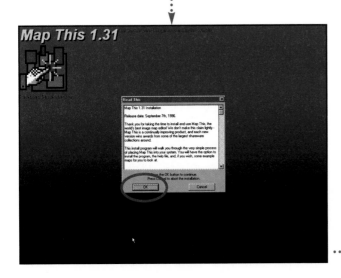

2 When the Read This dialogue box appears, click the **OK** button to continue the installation.

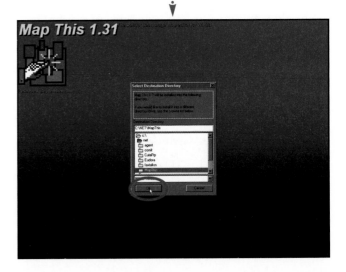

3 Next, select the directory in which you want to install Map This and click **OK**.

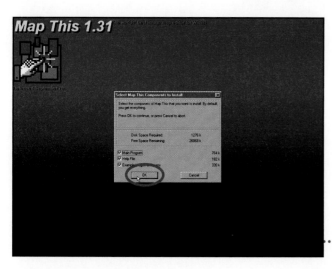

4 Now you must select which components of Map This you want to install. Make sure all the check boxes are marked and click **OK** to proceed.

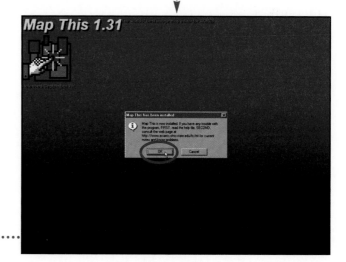

5 To finish the installation, click the **OK** button.

6 Now that you have the program installed, start it up. Go to the **Start** menu and select the **Map This** icon, which should be located under Programs.

7 Because you want to create a new imagemap, select **New** from the **File** menu.

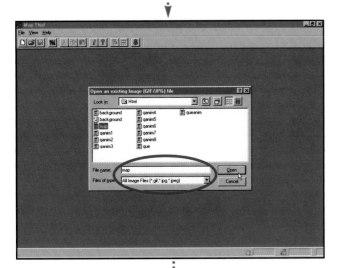

8 You will then be prompted for the location of the image file you want to use. Select the **map.gif** file, which is located in the Html directory.

Puzzled?

The map.gif file that you use in this part is a graphic I created (using Adobe Photoshop) for demonstration purposes. To complete the tasks regarding imagemaps, you need to acquire your own GIF or JPG image.

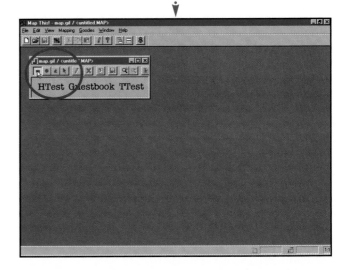

9 Next, to declare the active areas on your graphic, select the blue rectangle on the left-hand side of the toolbar. This tool lets you create active areas in your image.

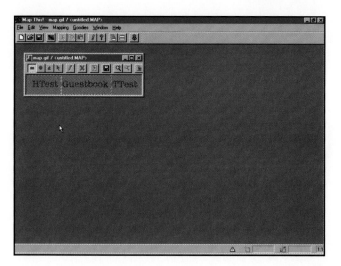

10 Finally, use the rectangle tool to draw rectangles, covering the three different areas that you want to activate. You are defining hot areas to which you will assign hyperlinks in the next task. ■

Adding Links to Active Areas

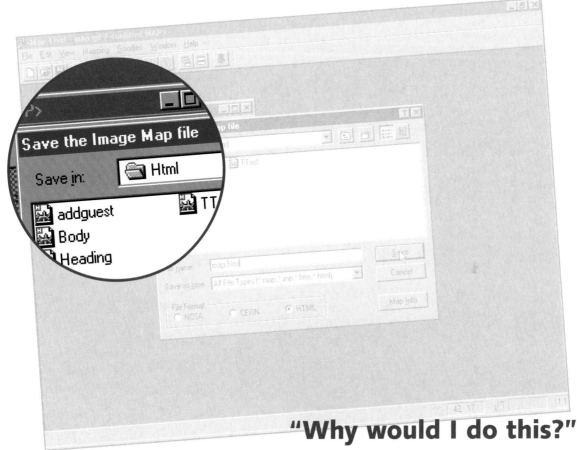

"Why would I do this?"

The whole purpose of an imagemap is for *graphical navigation* (in other words, to navigate the Web with pictures instead of regular text links). Making an imagemap without links is like trying to make a peanut butter and jelly sandwich without peanut butter and jelly.

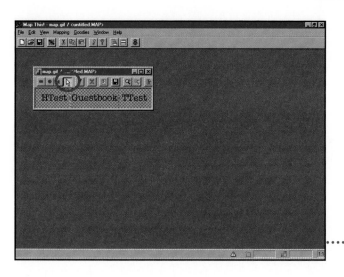

1 Adding links is simple: first, select the **arrow** button from the toolbar. The arrow tool enables you to add hyperlinks to your active areas.

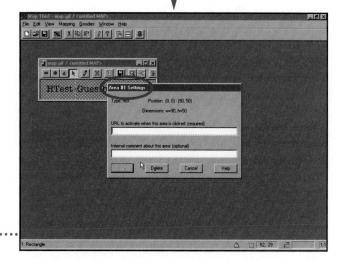

2 Then, double-click the area you want to *activate* (to assign a link to) first. The Area #1 Settings dialog box will be displayed.

3 Next, when the area is selected, enter the URL you want to access—in this case, htest.html. You can also add an internal comment for the link, though it is not necessary.

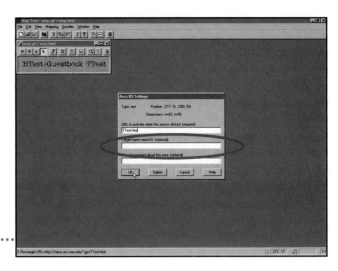

4 Double-click the second area and repeat the process for that area. The URL you use for this part is **http://www. webwareonline.com/developers/bgiel/ WWW/gbfiles/gbpub96-3381.html**, which is a link to your guestbook that you construct later.

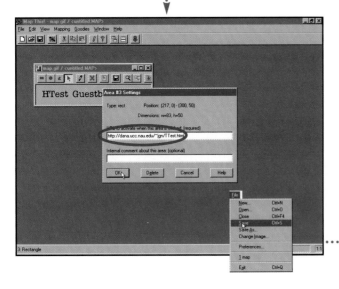

5 Since you want the last area to link to the table test page, double-click the third area and enter **TTest.html** in the URL box.

6 It is now time to save the file. Select **Save** from the **File** menu.

7 You will now be prompted with a new window. Enter the map's title (you will call it "mymap"), your name, and a default URL. This URL is used only when a section of the map that was not covered by your active areas is selected. You will use your index.html file as the default URL for this map. Click the **OK** button to continue.

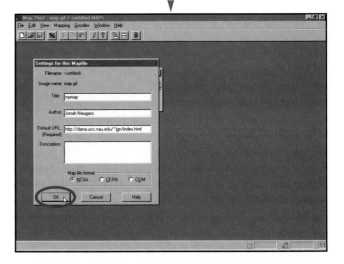

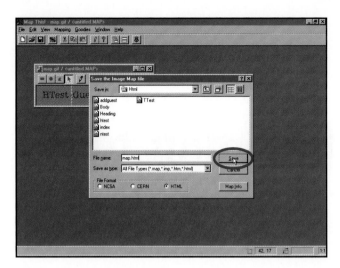

8 To end this task, select the HTML file for-mat and save it as **map.html**. Finally, select **Save**. ∎

Adding the Imagemap to Your Page

"Why would I do this?"

This is the point you have been building up to for the last few tasks. You will have a working imagemap on your page very soon!

1 Start WordPad and open the file map.html in the Html directory. You want to first take a look at what the imagemap does. There is the <map> tag, which declares the map and names it. Second, notice all of the lines beginning with <!-- #. These are comments that give information about the imagemap itself.

2 Notice all the lines starting with <AREA> (highlighted in the adjacent figure). These are what actually perform the magic of imagemaps. Each entry tells the browser what shape the active areas are and their coordinates. Every entry also has an URL with which it is associated.

3 Highlight the code from the <map> tag to the </map> tag and copy it into memory by pressing **CTRL+C**.

4 Open the Body.html file and position the cursor after the `</dl>` tag. Next, paste the map code into the file.

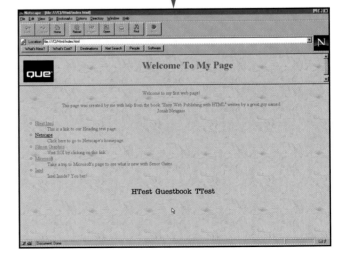

5 The last step in this process is adding the actual image that uses the imagemap code. Insert the following line after the `</map>` tag and save the file:

```
<center><img src="map.gif" usemap
➥="#mymap" align="center" border
➥=0></center>
```

6 Finally, load the index.html file in Netscape and see how your image-map looks. ■

Testing Your Imagemap

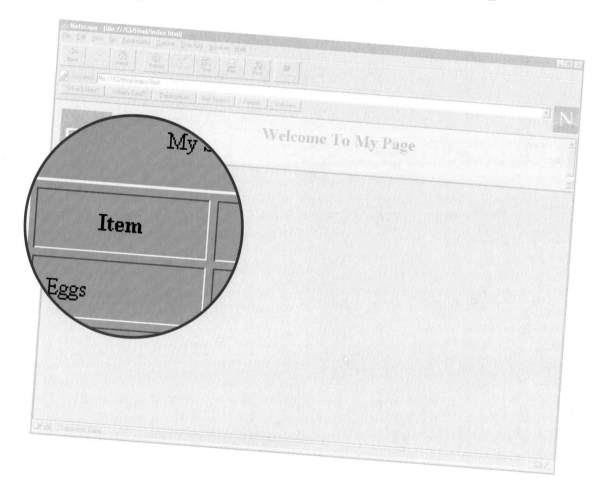

"Why would I do this?"

Like everything you have done in the previous sections, it is important that you test your imagemap. What you want to do is try each active area and see if it loads the files as you planned.

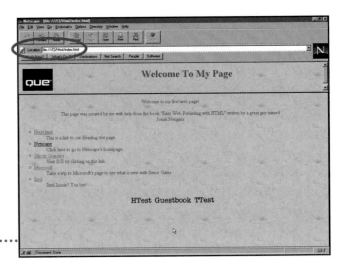

1 Load the index.html file in Netscape and scroll down to the bottom of the page, where your imagemap is.

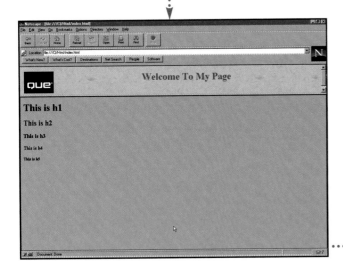

2 Click the HTest area of the map; it should take you to your heading test page.

3 Go back to the index file by pressing the **back** button on the toolbar. Select the TTest area of the map and you should be transported to your table test page. Congratulations, you did it! ■

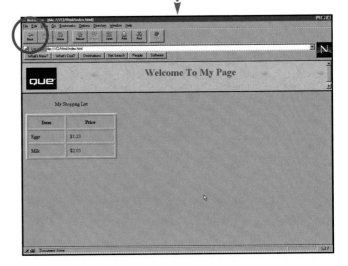

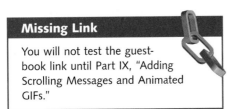

Missing Link

You will not test the guest-book link until Part IX, "Adding Scrolling Messages and Animated GIFs."

PART VIII

Uploading Your Web Page to Add Hit Counters and Guestbooks

FROM THIS POINT ON, you start getting into some of the more advanced HTML topics. The down side of this is that in order to perform some of these tasks, you need special access on the machine that serves your pages. To complete the tasks in this part you must have cgi-bin access on the machines on which your page resides; cgi-bin is a special directory that lets programs in languages such as Perl, C, and Visual Basic interact with your pages. Unfortunately, access to cgi-bin is often restricted because of security reasons. If you have any doubts as to whether you have cgi-bin access, ask your system administrator or service provider's technical support person. One of these two resources should be able to clear up any questions you may have.

The things you learn to do by following the tasks in this part not only add interest to your home page, but they let the surfer interact with your pages. For example, *hit counters* will tell you how many people have visited your site, while a *guestbook* lets a Web wanderer send input back to you.

You explore the Web for examples in this part and borrow them because these topics can be difficult to understand without research. Are you ready? Then buckle up, because you are going for a ride into the realm of advanced HTML.

Puzzled?

The first two lessons cover a program, CuteFTP32, which will show you how to transfer your HTML and CGI files to your service provider.

TASK

34

Downloading and Installing CuteFTP

"Why would I do this?"

The next few tasks of this part will cover using FTP to transfer your pages to the HTML directory on your service provider's system. After this transfer, your pages will actually become part of the Web and visible to Internet surfers around the world. To make your file transfers easier, you use an FTP program called CuteFTP32, one of the best FTP programs available. A quick note—CuteFTP32 is a 32-bit program and is made for Windows 95 or Windows NT. For Windows 3.1 users, there is also a 16-bit version of the program available.

Puzzled?

FTP stands for File Transfer Protocol and, as you may have guessed, is used for transferring files from one computer system to another.

1 In Netscape, if you go to **http://www. cuteftp.com/**, it will bring you to the CuteFTP home page. Click the link that says "Download CuteFTP."

2 Again, click the link that says "Download CuteFTP."

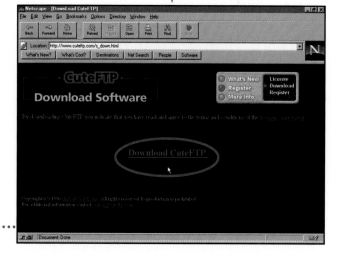

3 From the list of files, select **32cftp18.exe**. When the pop-up menu appears, select a directory in which to save the file. In this case, use your HTML directory.

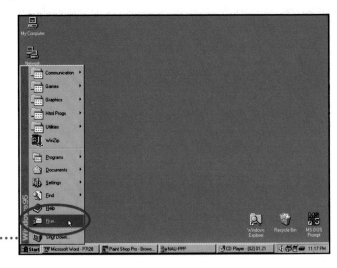

4 Time to install the program! Go to the **Start** menu and select **Run**.

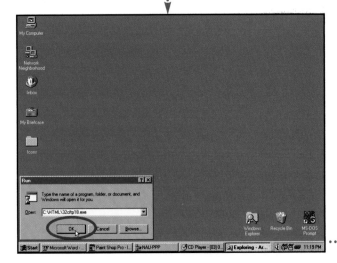

5 Enter the location of the CuteFTP archive (**C:\HTML\32cftp18.exe**) in the text box and follow the installation procedure.

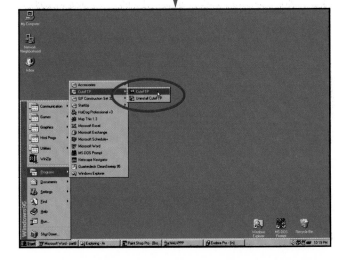

6 Start CuteFTP by going into the **Start** menu, **Programs**, **CuteFTP**, and selecting the **CuteFTP** icon.

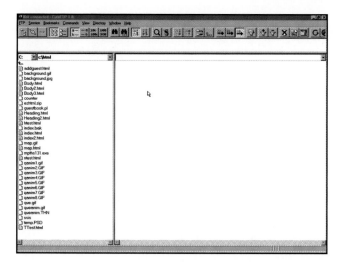

7 With CuteFTP started, you are ready to upload your page. ■

Uploading Your Web Page

"Why would I do this?"

You have come to a point where you are limited as to what you can test on your local machine. Some of the items you add in the next few lessons need the CGI support of your ISP (Internet Service Provider) to work. It's time to upload your pages to your ISP. For some of you, it may be an account on a school computer; others may have space with a commercial provider, such as America Online. To demonstrate, I upload your page to my school account. Your page's actual storage location may be different. If you are unsure about this location, contact your ISP for more information.

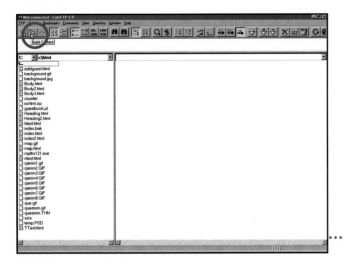

1 Click the **lightning bolt** symbol on the CuteFTP toolbar. This will bring up the Quick Connect dialog box.

Missing Link

If for some reason you do not yet have an HTML directory, contact your ISP for instructions on how to set one up.

2 In the **Quick Connect** menu, enter the address of the machine where you want to store your home page, as well as your login and password (your ISP will have given you this information). Click **OK** to initiate the connection.

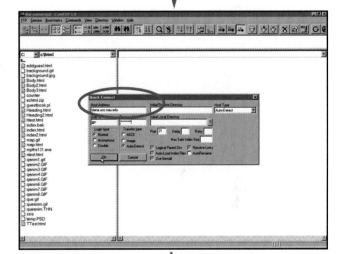

Missing Link

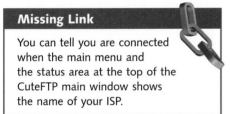

You can tell you are connected when the main menu and the status area at the top of the CuteFTP main window shows the name of your ISP.

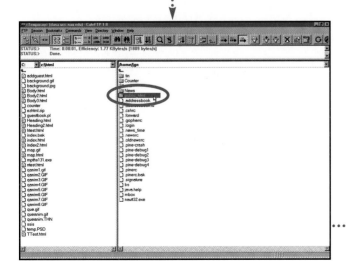

3 The CuteFTP screen is divided into two halves: the left window shows your local hard drive, the right, your ISP's home directory. Change to the HTML directory provided by your ISP by double-clicking the correct folder (public_html, in my case) in the right-hand window.

Task 35: Uploading Your Web Page

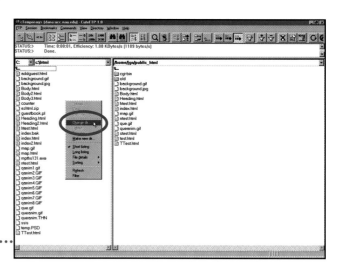

4 In order to transfer your HTML files to your ISP, they must be shown in the right pane of the CuteFTP window. You can change to the directory where your pages reside—in this case C:\html—by clicking the right mouse button in the left window and selecting the **Change dir** option.

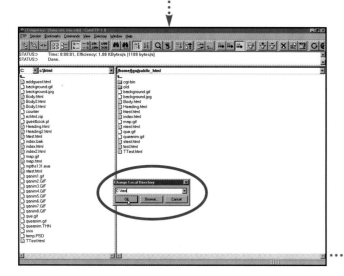

5 Now enter **C:\html** into the Change Local Directory box. This should make visible all the files you have created so far.

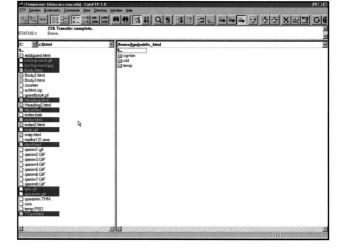

6 Select all the files you want to upload by pressing **CTRL** and clicking them with the mouse.

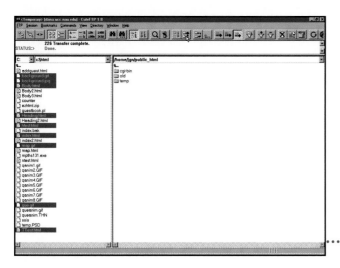

7 Next, click the **upload** button on the toolbar (it is the button with the arrow pointing up). This will transfer all the selected files from your local machine to your ISP, making them all available on the Web.

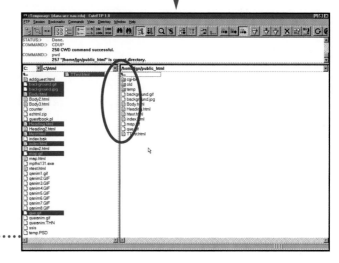

8 After the transfer is complete, all of the files you selected should appear in the right window.

9 Go to Netscape and put in your home page's URL. In this case it is **http://dana.ucc.nau.edu/~jgn**. There you have it! Your page is now online. ■

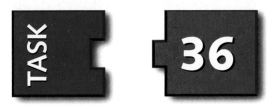

Getting the Software for a Hit Counter

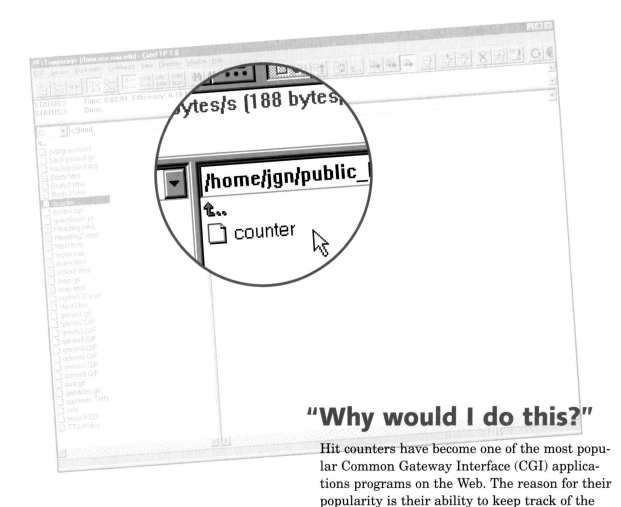

"Why would I do this?"

Hit counters have become one of the most popular Common Gateway Interface (CGI) applications programs on the Web. The reason for their popularity is their ability to keep track of the number of visits to a Web page, letting the page author know how well received his or her work is. For your purposes, you use a counter that is not only public domain, but fairly simple to install.

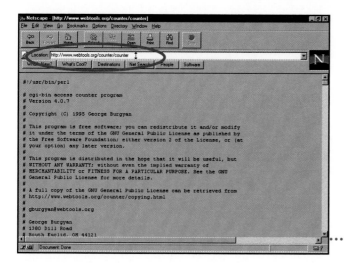

1 In Netscape, connect to **http://www.webtools.org/counter/counter**. This is the Perl program that you use for your counter.

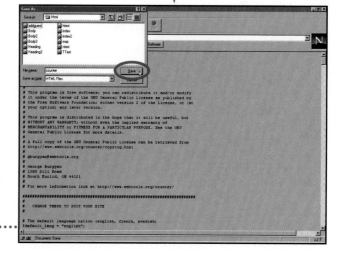

2 In the **File** menu, select **Save As**, and store the file in your HTML directory as **counter**.

3 Next, you must upload the counter program to your server. Connect to the server with CuteFTP and change to the cgi-bin directory on the remote machine (it may be different from your HTML directory). If you don't know where this directory is, ask your system administrator.

Task 36: Getting the Software for a Hit Counter

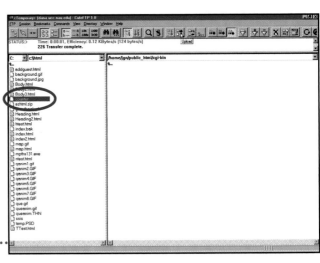

4 Change to your HTML directory on your local machine (left panel). Select the counter file and click the upload button.

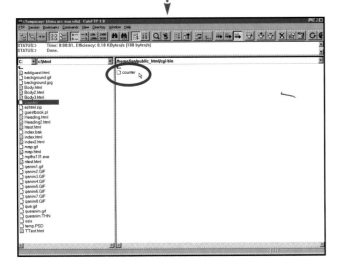

5 The counter file should now be in your cgi-bin directory on your ISP. ■

Installing the Hit Counter

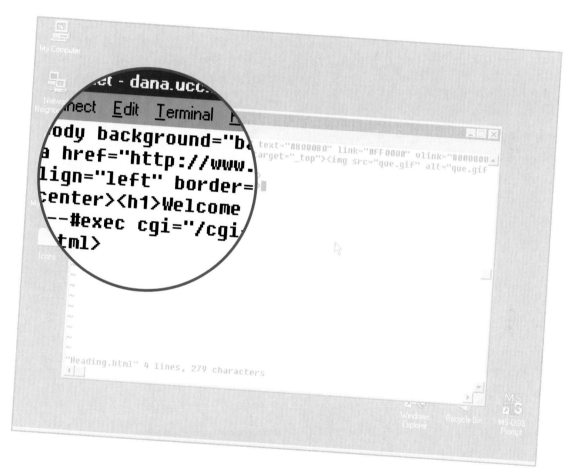

"Why would I do this?"

You have downloaded a counter program, but several steps need to be taken to get the counter working. First, you must slightly alter the counter file on your home system and upload the file again. Second, you must run a simple installation procedure on your host machine. Third, you must add a short reference to the counter in your HTML files.

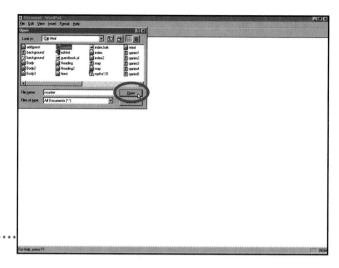

1 Open WordPad and load the file named counter. It is located in the HTML directory.

2 To run the counter program, your ISP must have Perl installed. Call your ISP for the availability and location (or path) of the Perl program as it varies from system to system (on my machine, it is in the "/nau/share/bin/" directory). Alter the first line so that it points to the Perl program's location on your host machine. In my case, I insert **#!/nau/share/bin/perl**. You need to keep the first two symbols (#!) in front of the path for the program to work correctly. Save the file as a text document after you have made the changes.

3 Follow the steps from the previous task to upload the modified counter file to the cgi-bin directory on your host machine.

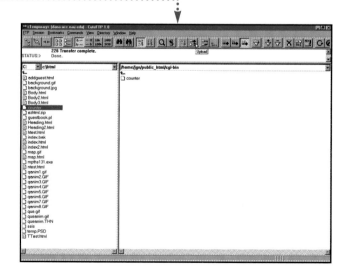

Puzzled?

The next few steps require the use of a program called "Telnet." Telnet enables you to connect to another machine and use that machine to perform tasks. These tasks may include programming, viewing text files, or even transferring files. In this case, you use Telnet to install the counter program on your machine.

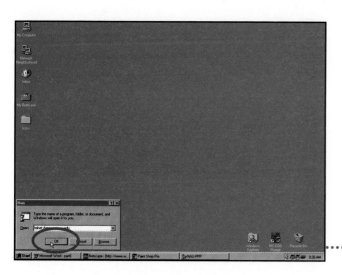

4 In the **Start** menu, select **Run**. Enter **telnet**, plus the name of your service provider. This will make a connection to your ISP (where your HTML and counter files are located), so that you can continue the installation procedure.

5 Log in to the machine using your login and password (your ISP sign-on may look different).

Missing Link

If part of the installation procedure did not work, refer to the counter installation guide at **http://www.webtools. org/counter/ installation.html**. Help from the system administrator may be needed.

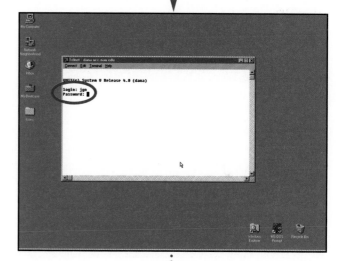

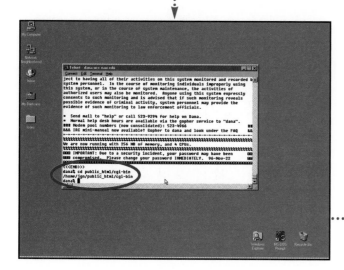

6 Now, change to the cgi-bin directory's location on the machine using the **cd** command (change directory), followed by the path to your cgi-bin directory. In my case, I would enter **cd public_html/cgi-bin**, followed by the enter key.

7 Type **Perl counter -install** at the command prompt to run the actual program. You should see the following text:

```
Installing the counter...
    ...making counter executable
    ...making link from counter to
    ➥counter-ord
    ...making link from counter to
    ➥counterfiglet
    ...making link from counter to
    ➥counterfiglet-ord
    ...making link from counter to
    ➥counterbanner
    ...making link from counter to
    ➥counterbanner-ord
...done!
```

8 To test the program's ability to work locally, enter **./counter**. You should get output that looks something like this:

```
Content-type: text/html

<a href="http://www.webtools.org/
➥counter/">1</a>
```

The number that appears before the </a> tag actually depends on how many times you have run the counter program. So, if you run it a second time, a 2 should appear instead of a 1!

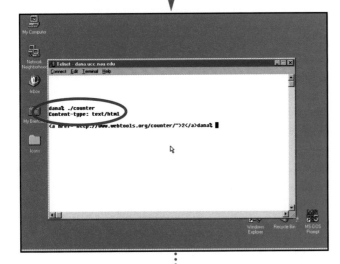

9 Open the Heading.html file in WordPad to add the reference to the counter in your HTML file. Insert the following line right after the </h1> tag:

```
<!--#exec cgi="/cgi-bin/counter"-->
```

Upload Heading.html to the HTML directory on your ISP and there you have it! ■

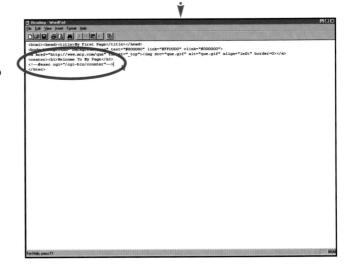

TASK

38

Registering for an Online Guestbook

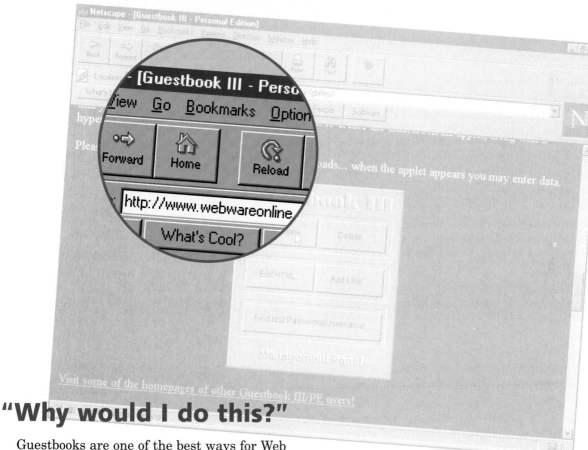

"Why would I do this?"

Guestbooks are one of the best ways for Web surfers to provide Web developers with input. The problem is that some guestbooks require knowledge of CGI programming and the use of HTML forms. There are, however, several companies on the Web that offer free guestbook services for personal pages. If you don't have cgi-bin access, using these services is the only way to get a guestbook up and running.

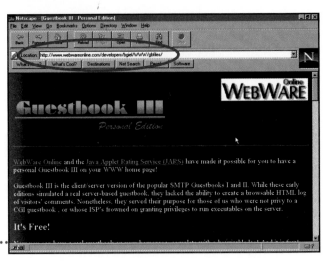

1 You use the services of a company called WebWare Online during this task. They offer free guestbook services with an easy-to-use Java interface. To get started, load **http://www.webwareonline.com/ developers/bgiel/WWW/gbfiles/** in Netscape.

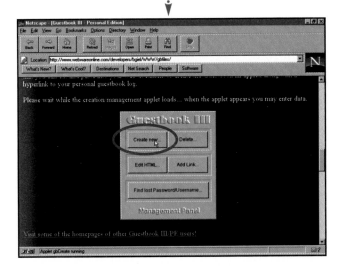

2 Scroll down until you get to the "Guestbook III Management Panel" and click the **Create New** button. A "New Guestbook" Java applet will be displayed. Enter your e-mail address, your home page's URL, your page's title, a username, and a password. This will provide the system with the information needed to send you further instructions. When you are finished, click the **Submit** button. If you accept the user agreement, you will be presented with a dialog box that tells you further instructions will be sent by e-mail. Congratulations, you have taken the first step in making your new guestbook! ■

Making the Guestbook Work

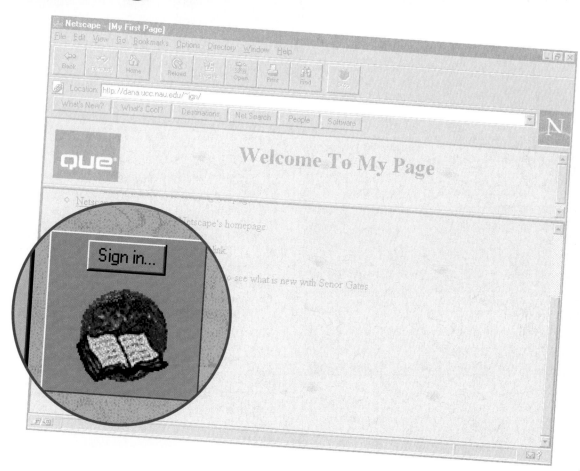

"Why would I do this?"

Now that you have an online guestbook, you
have to get it working. This involves copying
some code from the WebWare Online mail
message and pasting it into your HTML file.

1 In the **Start** menu, select **Run**. Enter **telnet**, plus the name of your service provider. Again, this will make a connection so that you can continue the installation procedure.

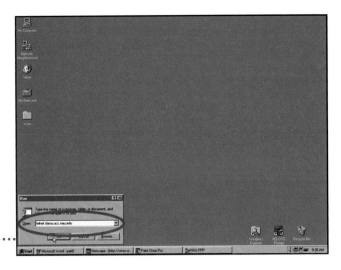

2 You should have a new message from Webmaster@jars.com entitled "Your Personal Guestbook." View the message and highlight the section of code starting with the `<applet>` tag and ending with `</applet>`. Then select **Copy** from the **Edit** menu.

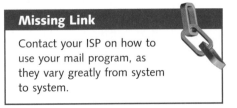

Missing Link

Contact your ISP on how to use your mail program, as they vary greatly from system to system.

3 Open the Body.html file with WordPad and position the cursor on the line after the `</dl>` tag.

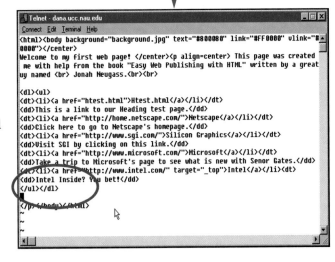

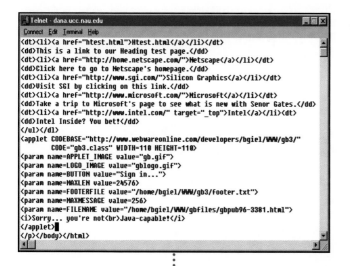

4 Select **Paste** from the **Edit** menu. This will copy the code necessary for your Guestbook to work. Save the file.

> **Missing Link**
>
> The guestbook you are using is actually a Java program. This means that only users with Java-enhanced browsers will be able to make entries in your guestbook. In addition, all the entries made are stored on the WebWare Online computer system. This means that if for some reason their system goes down, so does your guestbook.

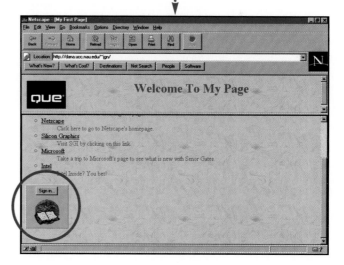

5 Now load the index.html file on the server so you can see if the insertion of your counter worked. You should see a gray box at the bottom of the page with a picture of a book, accompanied by a button that says Sign in. ■

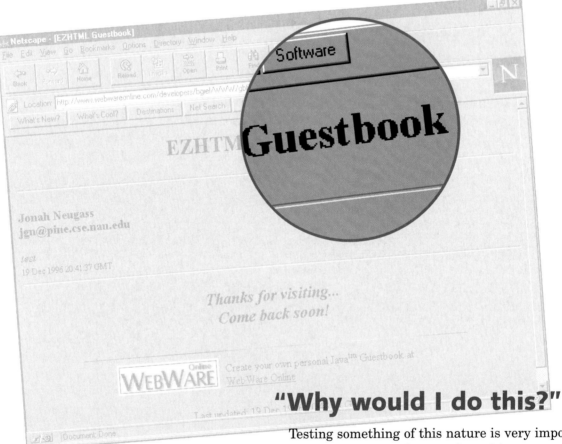

Testing the Guestbook

"Why would I do this?"

Testing something of this nature is very important. Having something such as this on your page that doesn't work looks very unprofessional. Quick note: if you don't have a Java-compatible browser you will be provided with a message that says Sorry...you're not Java-capable!. This means that you won't be able to test the guestbook. The same goes for visitors to your page with non-Java browsers. If everything is working correctly, however, you should have a small Java applet in the bottom left corner of your screen with a button labeled "Sign in" and a picture of an open book.

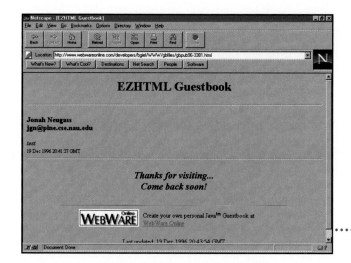

1 To test the guestbook, click the **Sign-in** button and fill in the text areas with your name, e-mail, and the word **test** for optional comments. After you are through, click the **Send** button.

2 To see if your submission worked, visit the URL provided to you in the e-mail from WebWare Online. In this case, it is **http://www.webwareonline.com/ developers/bgiel/WWW/gbfiles/ gbpub96-3381.html**. Once the page has loaded, you should see your submission as the first entry in your new guestbook! ■

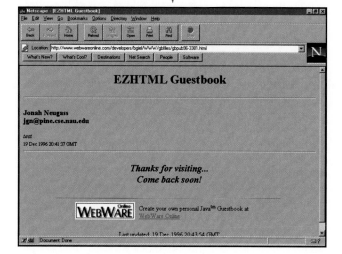

PART IX

Adding Scrolling Messages and Animated GIFs

WITH THE ADVENT OF BROWSER plug-ins (such as Real Audio, Shockwave, and the like), surfing the Internet has become much more exciting. However, there are problems with these add-on programs. First of all, some of these browser extensions can be quite sizable, and can take a long time to download. Also, there is not a strictly-set standard, so you may find several plug-ins that do relatively the same thing, but are not compatible. While these issues may not seem very important, they might discourage surfers who want to browse pages without a lot of hassle.

Luckily, most major Web browsers have incorporated two components into their programs to give users cool effects without the hassle. These two nifty items are JavaScript and animated GIFs. JavaScript is based on the now-popular programming language Java. Unlike Java, which requires entire programs residing on the host machine, JavaScript is included in the actual HTML code. While JavaScript is not as powerful as its big brother (Java), it is much easier to use. In addition, there are many examples on the Web that you can cut and paste into your own pages.

Until recently, animation on HTML pages was relatively unheard of. This has changed with the arrival of animated GIFs. An animated GIF is a series of GIFs played in sequence in order to create a "moving picture." In this way, these GIFs work almost like a "flip-book" or a cartoon. Luckily, there are a variety of programs available on the Web that help you construct animated GIFs.

This part will introduce you to some resources for both JavaScript and animated GIFs, as well as help you get those groovy features working on your own pages.

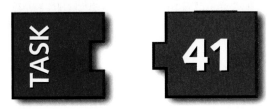

Copying an Example of JavaScript Scrolling Text

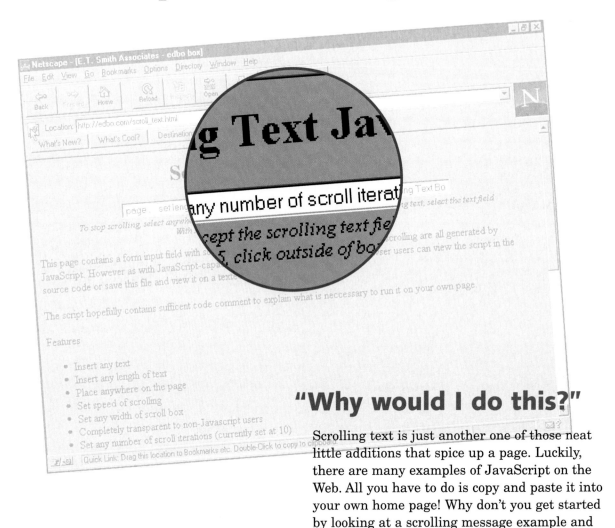

"Why would I do this?"

Scrolling text is just another one of those neat little additions that spice up a page. Luckily, there are many examples of JavaScript on the Web. All you have to do is copy and paste it into your own home page! Why don't you get started by looking at a scrolling message example and the code that creates it.

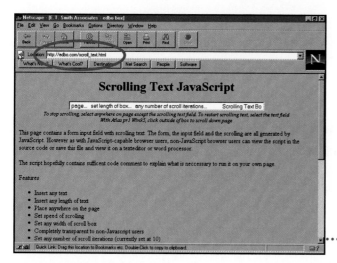

invalid link!

1 In Netscape, connect to **http://edbo.com/ scroll_text.html**. This is where you find your JavaScript example.

2 In the **View** menu, select **Document Source**. This will bring up the page's actual HTML code.

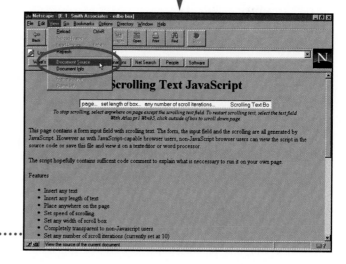

3 Highlight the entire JavaScript entry starting with <script> and ending with </script>. Press **CTRL+C** to copy the selected text into memory. ■

Inserting JavaScript into Your HTML File

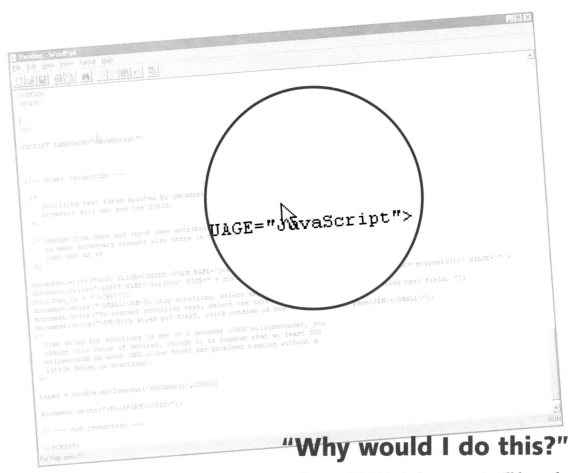

"Why would I do this?"

To complete this task you must still have the JavaScript (acquired in the last task) in memory. If not, redo Task 41, as you will have to paste the JavaScript in memory into your HTML code.

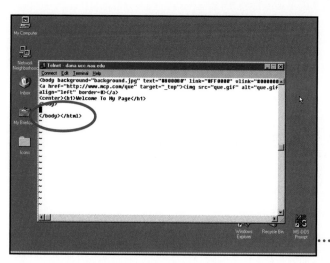

1 Start WordPad and open the Heading.html file for editing. Open a line right before the </body> tag. This is where you insert your JavaScript.

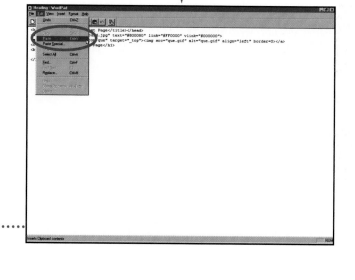

2 Select **Paste** in the **Edit** menu to paste the script into your file.

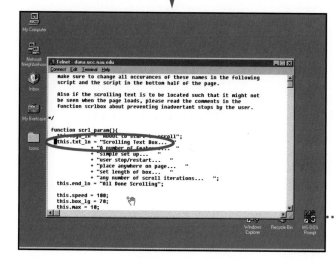

3 Now you need to update the script to match your page. First, scroll up until you reach a line that reads:

```
this.txt_ln = "Scrolling Text
➥Box...   "
```

This is the beginning of the area that specifies what text will scroll across the screen.

4 Change the entry to the following:

```
this.txt_ln = "Welcome To My
➥Page...    "
              + "This page is an
                  ➥example...    "
              + "of what can be
                  ➥accomplished...    "
              + "with the book...    "
              + "Easy Web Publishing
                  ➥with HTML...    ";
```

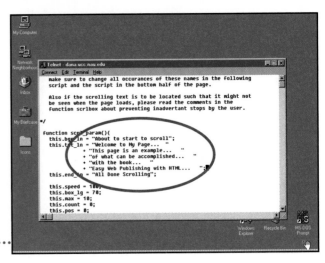

5 Next, scroll down the page until you find the line that reads:

```
<H1 ALIGN="CENTER">Scrolling Text
➥JavaScript</H1>
```

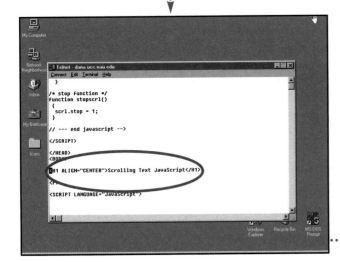

6 As you already have a heading, you don't need this one. Delete the entire line and save the file. On to testing! ■

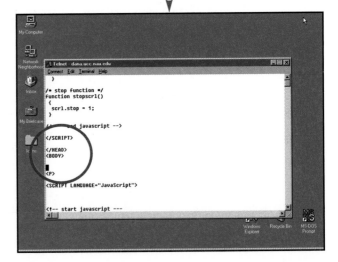

Testing the JavaScript

"Why would I do this?"

Time for testing! Let's link to your new Web page with the added scrolling code and see if it works!

1 Before you can test the JavaScript counter, you must first upload the updated Heading.html to your ISP. Connect to your ISP using CuteFTP and change to the HTML directory.

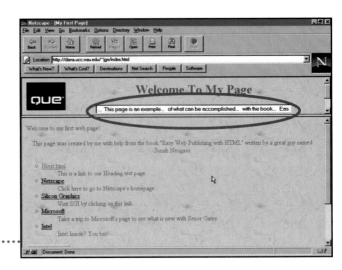

2 Select the **Heading.html** file in the left window pane and click the **Upload** button. This will upload your file with the newly-added JavaScript.

3 Start Netscape and enter your home page's URL.

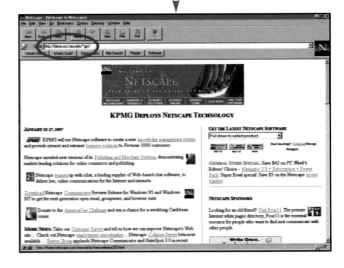

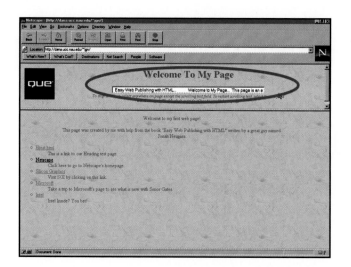

4 Your updated page should appear. You should see a box with your scrolling text in your heading area! ∎

Puzzled?

If you don't see the scrolling text, make sure that JavaScript is turned on in the Network Preferences menu. If you still have problems seeing the scrolling text, try clearing your memory and disk cache and reloading your home page.

Finding and Downloading a GIF Animation Program

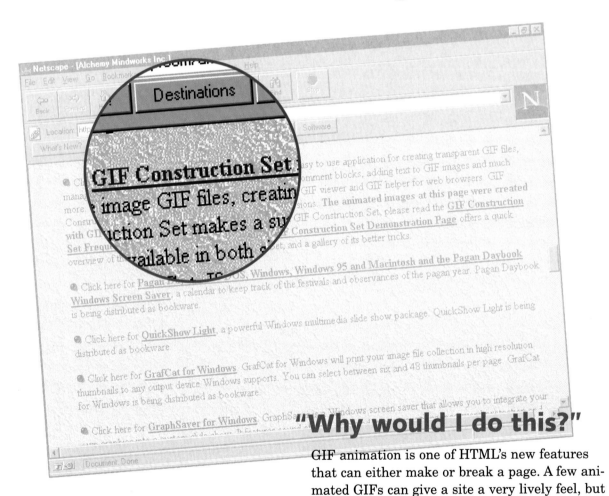

"Why would I do this?"

GIF animation is one of HTML's new features that can either make or break a page. A few animated GIFs can give a site a very lively feel, but too many and the page becomes chaotic. You use a program called the "GIF Construction Set" from Alchemy Mindworks, Inc. to animate your GIFs. Like most of the other programs you have used so far, it is available on the Web.

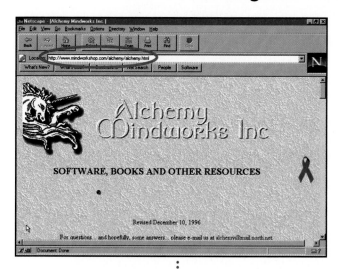

1 To get to the Alchemy Mindworks home page, load the following in Netscape: **http://www.mindworkshop.com/alchemy/alchemy.html**.

Missing Link

Programs for building animated GIFs are also available for the Macintosh. One such program, entitled "GifBuilder", may be found at **http://iawww.epfl.ch/Staff/Yves.Piguet/clip2gif-home/GifBuilder.html**.

2 Scroll down the page until you find a link for the GIF Construction Set and click it.

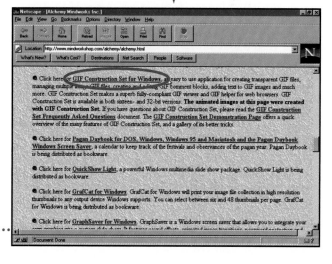

3 When the pop-up menu appears, change to the HTML directory and press **Save**. This should initiate the GIF Construction Set download. This may take a while, depending on the speed of your connection; it will be on your hard drive, ready for installation, when it is done. ∎

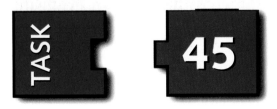

Creating an Animated GIF

"Why would I do this?"

Now that you have the downloaded installation file for your GIF animator program, it is time to install the GIF Construction Set and begin animating.

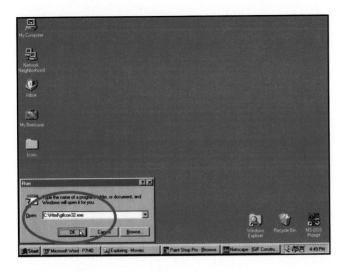

1 Go to the **Start** menu and select **Run**. Enter **C:\Html\gifcon32.exe** and click **OK**. Follow the installation instructions.

Puzzled?

An animated GIF works much like a cartoon does. A cartoon is a series of drawings that mimic live action. These sequences, when flashed quickly across the screen, create movement. An animated GIF is a series of picture files that, when shown quickly in order, creates an animated affect. To complete this task, you must have a series of GIFs in a logical sequence.

2 The installation procedure should create a program group. Double-click the **GIF Construction Set 32** icon to start the program.

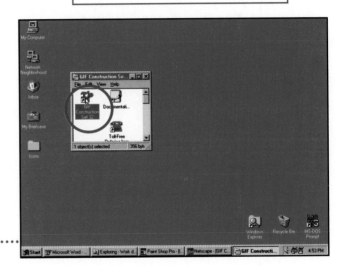

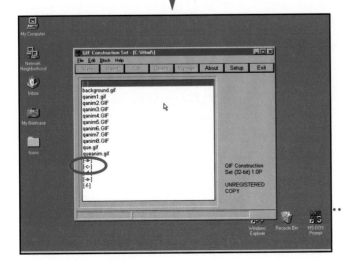

3 Once the program is loaded, change to the directory where you have your GIF files. In this case, you change to the Html directory by double-clicking on **[-c-]**, then **Html**.

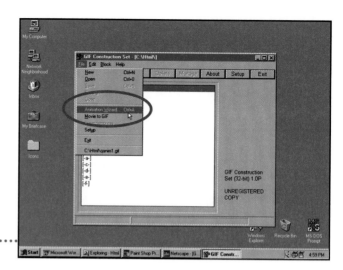

4 Go to the **File** menu and select **Animation Wizard**.

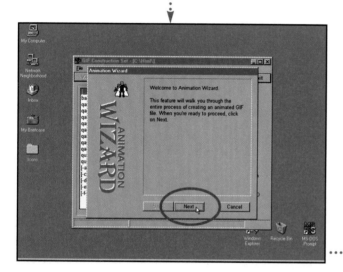

5 Make sure that the **Yes, for use with a Web Page** is selected and press **Next**. Select **Next** from the first screen.

6 Check the **Loop indefinitely** option and click **Next**. The "Loop indefinitely" option means the GIF will continue playing until your page's viewer presses the stop button. Without this, the GIF will play once and stop.

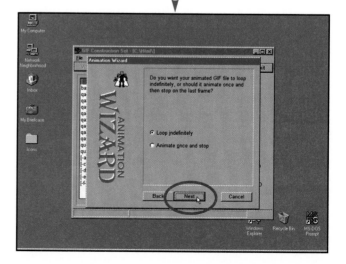

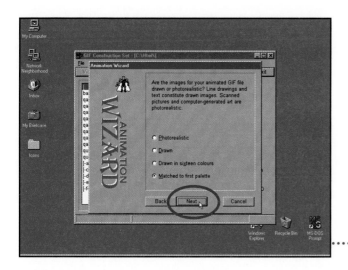

7 In this case, select **Matched to first palette** and then select **Next**. This will dither all of the GIFs to the same 256 color palette as the first image in the series.

8 Now it is time to choose a *delay* for your GIF. The delay is the time in between each animation frame. If you want a fast animation, use a short delay. If you want a slow animation, use a long delay. In this case, use the default delay for your animation. Press **Next** to continue.

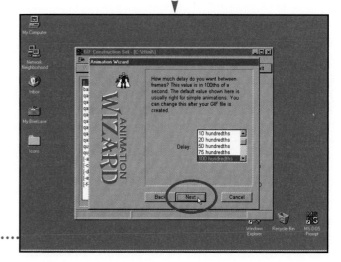

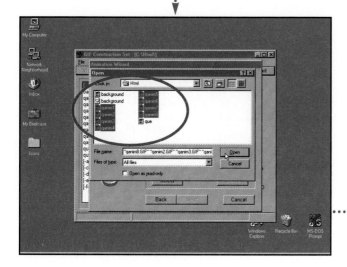

9 Now select the GIF files to put in your animation. Press the **Select** button and highlight all the files that will be used. Hit the **Open** button.

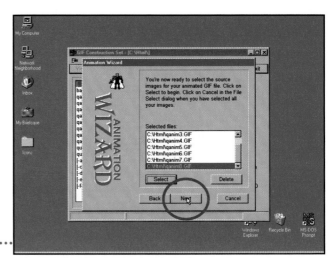

10 Again, click the **Next** button. This tells the program that you are done selecting image files.

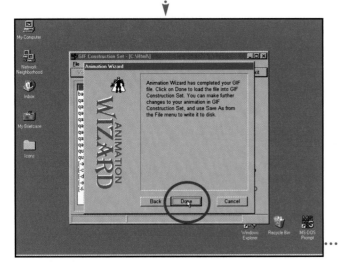

11 To finish setting up your animated GIF, press **Done**. All the steps to create an animated GIF are complete.

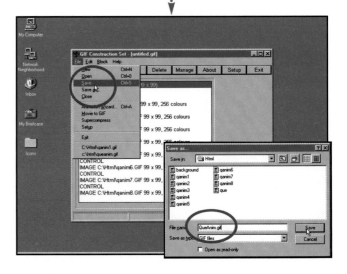

12 All that is left is saving the file. Go to the **File** menu and select **Save as**.

13 Enter **QueAnim.gif** for the filename and press the **Save** button. There you have it: your own animated GIF! ■

Inserting the Animated GIF into the HTML File

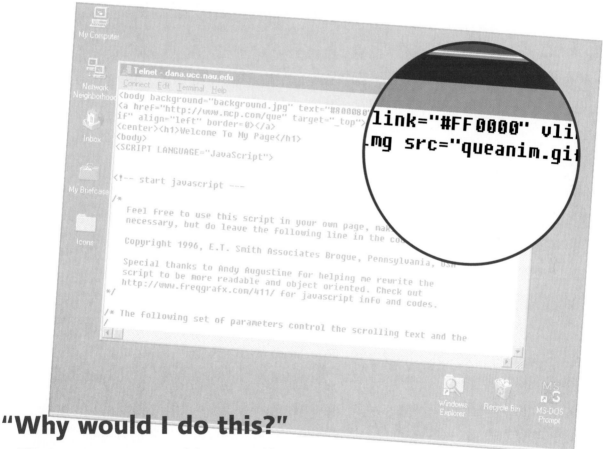

"Why would I do this?"

This is an important part of the process if you want your GIF to be seen. Luckily, the procedure is simple. An animated GIF is added just like any other picture (with the <img> tag).

Task 46: Inserting the Animated GIF into the HTML File

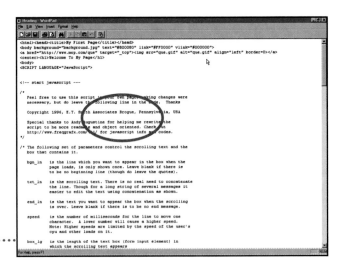

1 Open the **Heading.html** file in WordPad.

2 To include your new animated GIF, replace all references to "que.gif" in the <img> tag with **queanim.gif**. Save the file.

3 Now you must connect to your ISP using CuteFTP. Click the **Lightning Bolt** icon and enter your login information.

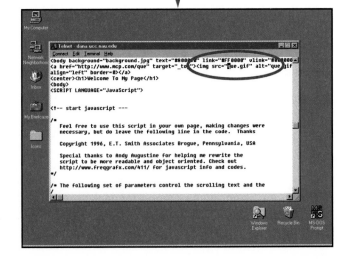

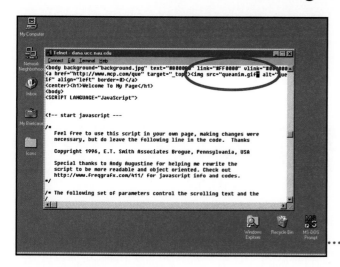

4 Change to your HTML directory by double-clicking it in the right panel of CuteFTP.

5 Upload the animated GIF by selecting it in the left panel and clicking the **Upload** button. You are ready to test your new GIF. ■

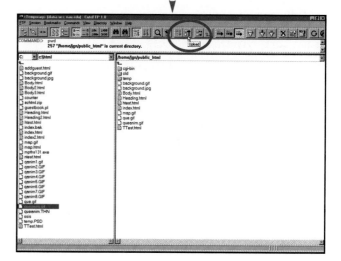

Testing Your Animated GIF

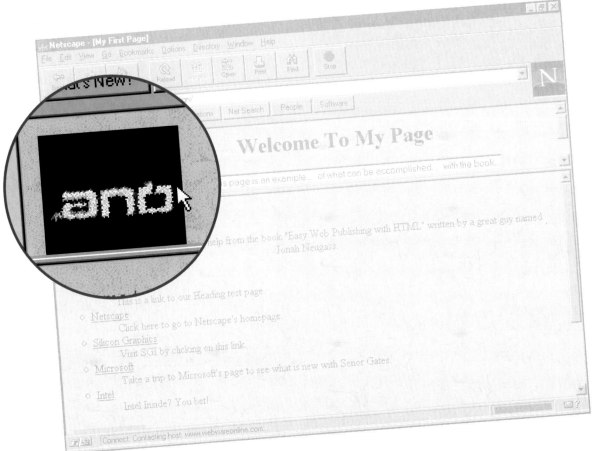

"Why would I do this?"

When you load your home page, you should
see the new GIF file doing its thing.

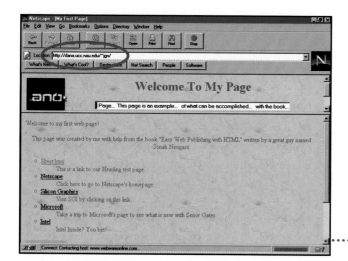

1 In Netscape, enter your home page's URL.

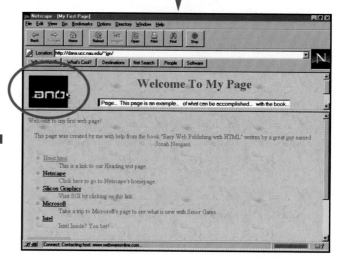

2 When the page is loaded, your GIF should be moving in a dance of animated pixels. ■

PART X

Web Site Creation Tools and Cool Web Sites

THERE ARE A HUGE NUMBER of Web site creation tools on the market today, and even more on the horizon. Luckily, a great number of them are either *shareware* or have a reasonable evaluation period.

These tools can make your life much easier with things like toolbars that contain commonly used tags, menus that will build tables for you, and much more. However, there is a slight drawback. After you use these programs for a while, they can become a crutch. Remember, HTML is like any other language: if you don't use it, you may forget it.

The first three tasks in this part cover some of the best HTML editors out there. Each task shows you where to go to download the program, as well as show you reviews for the program. Those reviews come from one of the best collections of Internet Applications on the Web: "Stroud's Consummate Apps List." These tasks only cover how to find and download these helper applications, not how to use them. For details on program use, please refer to each application's help files.

The last two tasks in this part show you two Web sites that stand above other, average Web pages you may come across. Out of over thirteen million Web sites, you would be surprised to find how many of them are just plain bad (definitely the majority). Task 53 points you to the Macmillan SuperLibrary, which is a great place to find more books and other sources of information on HTML books, as well as any other computer-related topic. Task 54 shows you a Web page displaying the table of colors with their hexadecimal value. That page will help you select the right color for your next great Web page.

> **Puzzled?**
>
> Shareware refers to programs that are almost free of charge; the program's author would like you to contribute money, but it is usually not required. Some shareware programs are *crippled* (missing features) and can only be enabled after the program is *registered* (paid for).

TASK

48

Downloading HomeSite for Windows 95

"Why would I do this?"

HomeSite offers a huge variety of tools and features including enhanced JavaScript support, link verification, and the latest tags. HomeSite also offers a *freeware* version in addition to their shareware version.

Puzzled?

Freeware is almost like shareware except for the fact that no fee is required to get a registered version of the program. Thus the name "freeware!"

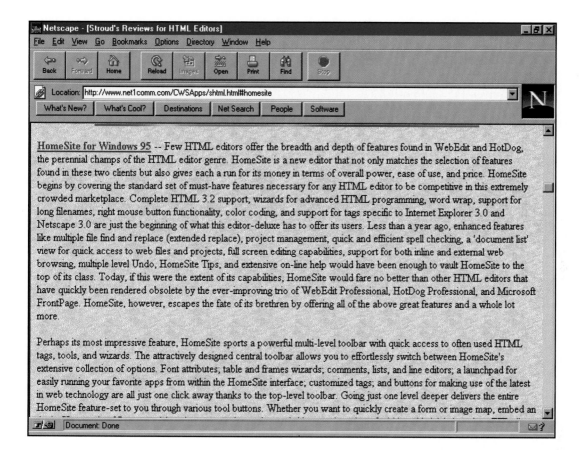

For the full review of HomeSite for Windows 95, go to **http://www.net1comm.com/CWSApps/shtml.html#homesite**.

You can download HomeSite by visiting their site at **http://www.dexnet.com/homesite.html** and clicking the **download** button in the menu.

When the Save As dialog box appears, save the hs12set file to a temporary directory (c:\temp, for example).

To start the installation procedure, select **Run** from the **Start** menu and enter **c:\temp\hs12set.exe**. Follow the online steps to complete the installation.

Downloading WebEdit

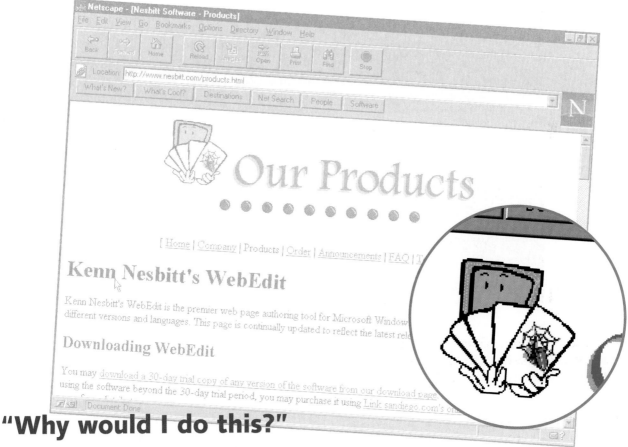

"Why would I do this?"

The new version of WebEdit gives the user
a veritable plethora of features, including a
built-in imagemap editor, FTP uploading, an
enhanced Web previewer, and even user-
defined tags. WebEdit also comes in two ver-
sions: the Professional and the Standard. As
you would guess, the Standard version costs
much less than the Professional (about half
the cost).

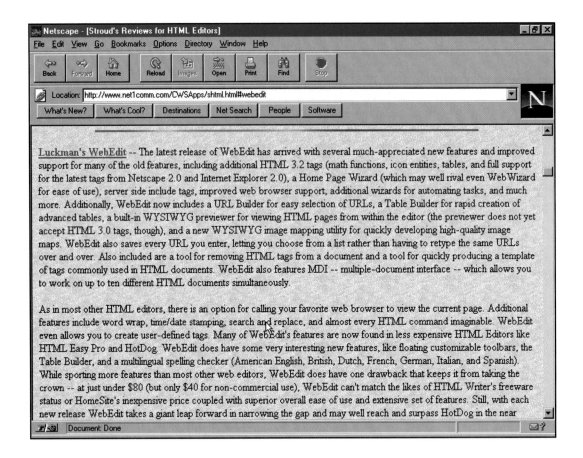

The review of WebEdit can be found at
**http://www.net1comm.com/CWSApps/
shtml.html#webedit**.

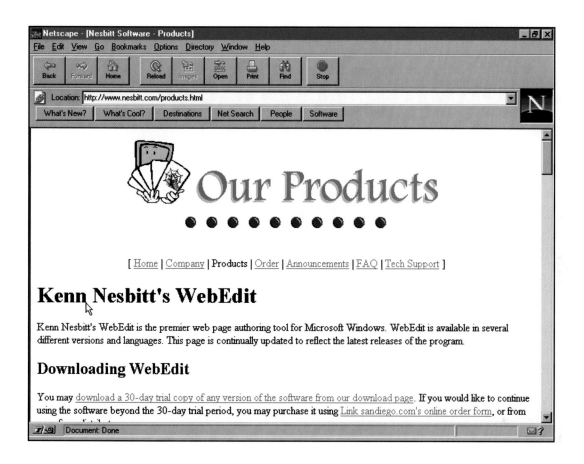

The WebEdit home page can be found at
http://www.nesbitt.com/products.html
and offers a 30-day trial copy of their software.

When the Save As dialog box appears, save the
we2std32 file to a temporary directory.

To install the application, UnZip the file to the
temporary directory, select **Run** from the **Start**
menu, and enter **c:\temp\setup.exe**. Follow
the online steps to complete the installation.

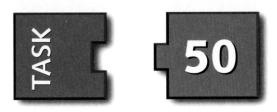

Downloading HTMLed 32-bit

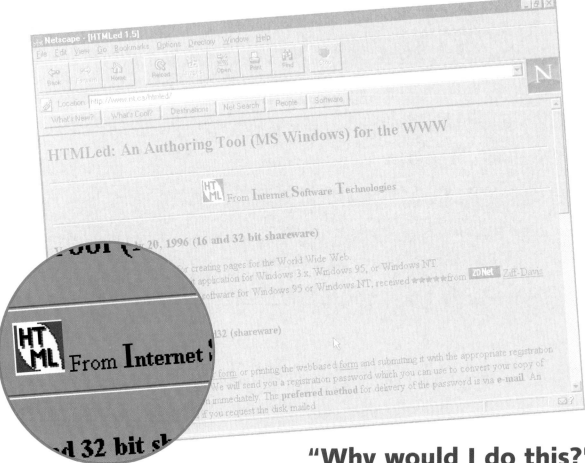

"Why would I do this?"

While it doesn't have as many features as the two previously mentioned products, HTMLed does have its good points. Those include ease of use, intelligent tagging, great table and form designers, and an integrated spell checker.

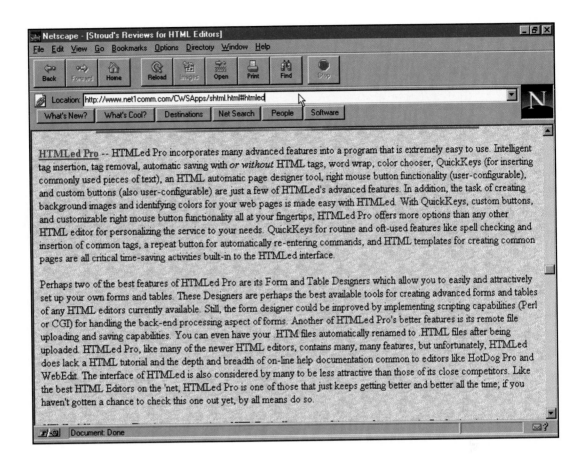

Stroud's review can be found at
**http://www.net1comm.com/CWSApps/
shtml.html#htmled**.

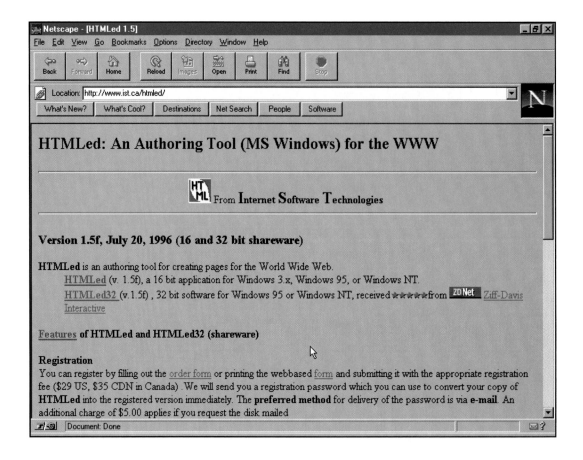

You can download HTMLed 32-bit at its home page: **http://www.ist.ca/htmled/**.

When the Save As dialog box appears, save the hte32_2s file to a temporary directory.

To start the installation procedure, select **Run** from the **Start** menu and enter **c:\temp\hte32_2s.exe**. Follow the online steps to complete the installation.

Downloading from TUCOWS and Stroud's

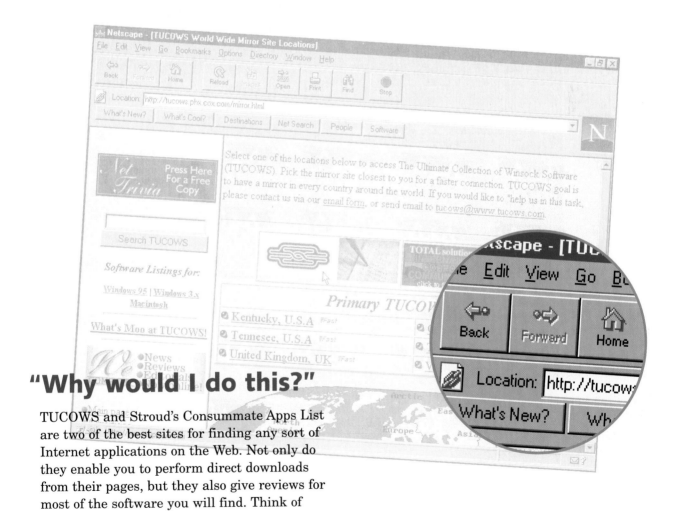

"Why would I do this?"

TUCOWS and Stroud's Consummate Apps List are two of the best sites for finding any sort of Internet applications on the Web. Not only do they enable you to perform direct downloads from their pages, but they also give reviews for most of the software you will find. Think of these two sites as a library of Internet applications. If you are interested in one of the programs, just download it as if you were checking out a book!

The main strength of Stroud's Consummate Apps List is the author's great reviews. Mr. Stroud has included reviews for every application that he has on his site. The list also has many mirror sites, so pick the one closest to you by visiting **http://www.net1comm.com/ CWSApps/cwsapps.html**.

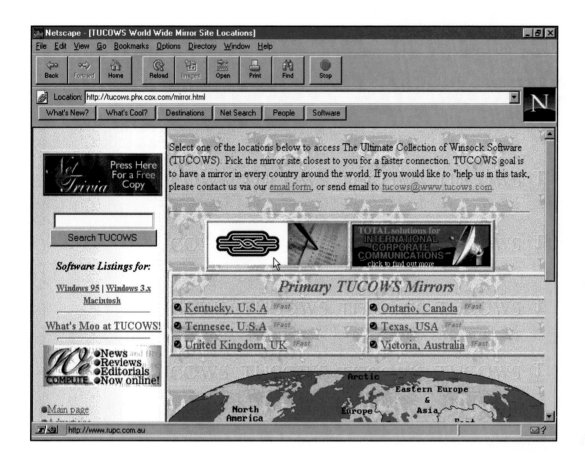

TUCOWS is a great site not only because of the huge variety of software available, but also because of its search engine (which makes applications easier to find), and the fact that it has over 140 mirror sites available all over the world. You can connect to any of the TUCOWS mirror sites by visiting this link: **http://tucows.phx.cox.com/mirror.html**.

TASK **52**

Accessing the Macmillan Information SuperLibrary

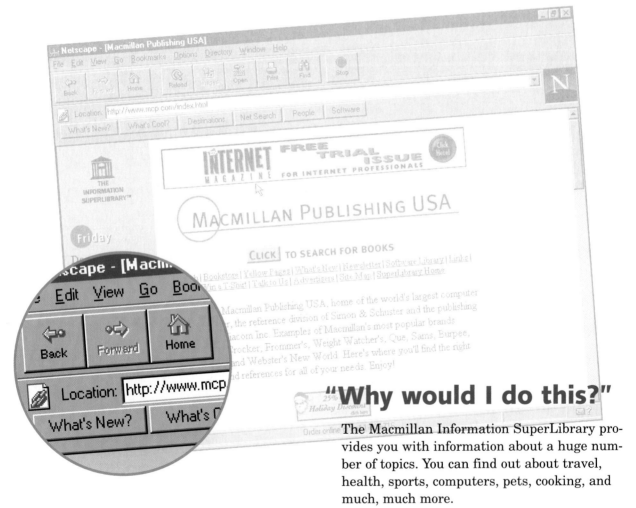

"Why would I do this?"

The Macmillan Information SuperLibrary provides you with information about a huge number of topics. You can find out about travel, health, sports, computers, pets, cooking, and much, much more.

Find a wealth of knowledge at **http://www. mcp.com/index.html**.

TASK 53

A Table of Colors in Hexadecimal

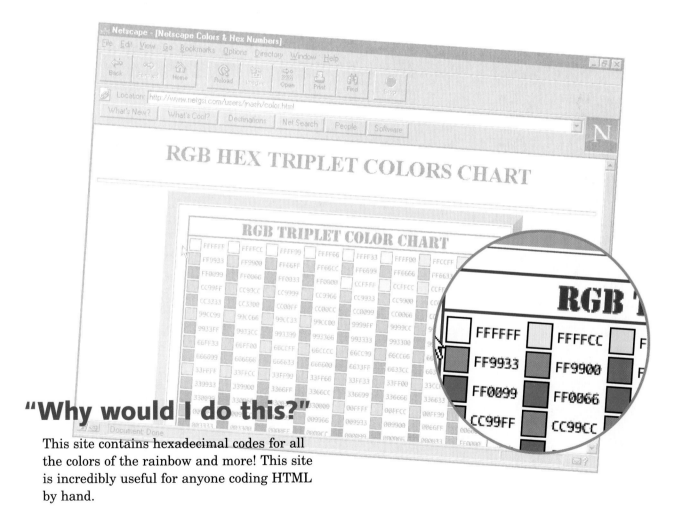

"Why would I do this?"

This site contains hexadecimal codes for all the colors of the rainbow and more! This site is incredibly useful for anyone coding HTML by hand.

Take a trip over the rainbow at **http://www.netgsi.com/users/jnash/color.html** and find the colors that you need to spice up your page.

Index

Symbols

/a tags, terminators, 33
/dl tags, cursors, positioning, 102
/HTML tags, adding, 79
/li tags, bulleted lists, 53
/p tags, relative links, adding, 35
/table tags, adding, 63

A

a href tags
    graphics, 47
    links, 33
absolute links
    adding, procedures, 37
    definition, 32
    purpose, 36
access, ogi bin, 106
accessing Macmillan Information
    SuperLibrary, 166
acquiring, software, hit counters,
    117-118
active areas
    imagemaps
        adding, 92-94
        purpose, 91
    links
        adding, 97-99
        features, 96
adding
    /HTML tags, 79
    /table tags, 63
    active areas, imagemaps, 92-94
    borders, tables, 65
    captions, tables, 69
    frames
        procedures, 79-81
        purpose, 78
        WordPad files, 80
    graphics
        procedures, 43
        purpose, 42

imagemaps
    procedures, 101
    purpose, 100
images, imagemaps, 102
links
    absolute, 37
    active areas, 97-99
    graphics, 15
modifiers, table tags, 67
noframetags, 81
relative links
    procedures, 35
    purpose, 34
tables
    headings, 74
    tags, 63
additional files, creating, 79
addresses, URLs, features, 32
align= tags, procedures, 20
aligning
    graphics
        procedures, 45
        purpose, 44
    text
        features, 19
        procedures, 20-21
Animated GIFs
    creating
        procedures, 143-146
        purpose, 142
    definition, 130
    downloading
        procedures, 141
        purpose, 140
    HTML
        features, 147
        inserting, 148-149
    testing
        procedures, 151
        purpose, 150
AREA tags, 101
arrow buttons, links, adding, 97, 99

B

b c buttons, 104
b tags
    features, 28
    text, emphasizing, 29-30
backgrounds
    colors
        changing, 23
        default, 22
    pictures
        features, 48
        inserting, 49
body tags, colors
    backgrounds, 23
    links, 39
    text, 25
borders, tables
    adding, 65
    features, 64
br tags
    creating, 16
    practicing, 17-18
    purpose, 15
bulleted lists
    creating, procedures, 53-54
    tags
        li, 53
        p align=, 54
        ul, 53
    purpose, 52

C

captions, tables
    adding, 69
    purpose, 68
cell padding
    changing, 70
    modifiers, table tags, 71
cell spacing

Index

backgrounds, 48
dithering, definition, 40
formats, standard, 40
imagemaps, definition, 86
links
a href tags, 47
adding, 47
features, 46
modifiers, img tags, 45
guestbooks
configuring
features, 125
procedures, 126-127
registering, 124
requirements, 123
testing
procedures, 129
purpose, 128

H

h1 tags, 13
h5 tags, 13
headings
tables, 73
tags
procedures, 12-14
purpose, 11
heights, tables
changing, 67
features, 66
hexadecimal codes, colors, 167
hit counters
features, 116
installing
procedures, 120-122
requirements, 119
software, acquiring, 117-118
home pages, imagemaps, downloading, 89-90
homesite
downloading, 155-156
features, 154
hot areas, defining, rectangle tools, 95
hr tags
features, 26
text
separating, 27
seperating, 27

HTML
animated GIFs
features, 147
inserting, 148-149
editors, 152
JavaScript
inserting, 135-136
requirements, 134
overview, 2
HTMLed
downloading, 162
features, 160
locating, 161
hyperlinks, see links
Hypertext Markup Language, *see* HTML

I

i tags
features, 28
text, emphasizing, 29-30
imagemaps
active areas
adding, 92-94
purpose, 91
adding
images, 102
procedures, 101
purpose, 100
codes, definition, 86
creating
new, 94
overview, 86
downloading
home pages, 89
procedures, 89-90
purpose, 88
files, selecting, 94
graphical button bars, 86
graphics, definition, 86
saving, 90
testing
procedures, 104
purpose, 103
images, adding, imagemaps, 102
img tags, modifiers, graphics, 45
inserting
animated GIFs, 148-149

JavaScript, 135-136
pictures, backgrounds, 49
terminators, tags, 81
installing
CuteFTP, 109-111
hit counters
procedures, 120-122
requirements, 119
Map, 92-93
ISPs (Internet Service Providers), CGI support, 112

J-K

JavaScript
HTML
inserting, 135-136
requirements, 134
overview, 130
scrolling text
copying, 133
definition, 132
testing
procedures, 138-139
purpose, 137
JPG files, 40
justifying text, 20-21

L

layout, frames, 76
learning tags
headers, 12-14
practice pages, 8-10
li tags, bulleted lists, 53
lightening bolt symbols, CuteFTP, 113-114
links
absolute
adding, 37
purpose, 36
active areas
adding, 97-99
features, 96
colors
changing, 39
features, 38
features, 32

Index

Check out Que® Books on the World Wide Web
http://www.quecorp.com

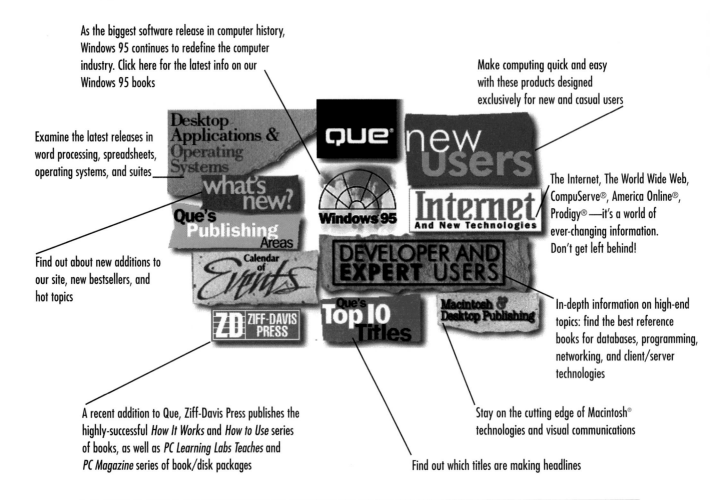

As the biggest software release in computer history, Windows 95 continues to redefine the computer industry. Click here for the latest info on our Windows 95 books

Make computing quick and easy with these products designed exclusively for new and casual users

Examine the latest releases in word processing, spreadsheets, operating systems, and suites

The Internet, The World Wide Web, CompuServe®, America Online®, Prodigy® —it's a world of ever-changing information. Don't get left behind!

Find out about new additions to our site, new bestsellers, and hot topics

In-depth information on high-end topics: find the best reference books for databases, programming, networking, and client/server technologies

A recent addition to Que, Ziff-Davis Press publishes the highly-successful *How It Works* and *How to Use* series of books, as well as *PC Learning Labs Teaches* and *PC Magazine* series of book/disk packages

Stay on the cutting edge of Macintosh® technologies and visual communications

Find out which titles are making headlines

With 6 separate publishing groups, Que develops products for many specific market segments and areas of computer technology. Explore our Web Site and you'll find information on best-selling titles, newly published titles, upcoming products, authors, and much more.

- Stay informed on the latest industry trends and products available
- Visit our online bookstore for the latest information and editions
- Download software from Que's library of the best shareware and freeware

Copyright © 1997, Macmillan Computer Publishing-USA, A Viacom Company

MACMILLAN COMPUTER PUBLISHING USA
A VIACOM COMPANY

Technical Support:

If you need assistance with the information in this book or with a CD/Disk
accompanying the book, please access the Knowledge Base on our Web
site at **http://www.superlibrary.com/general/support**. Our most
Frequently Asked Questions are answered there. If you do not find the
answer to your questions on our Web site, you may contact Macmillan
Technical Support **(317) 581-3833** or e-mail us at **support@mcp.com**.